U.S. ARMY VEHICLE MARKINGS 1944

Jean Bouchery and Philippe Charbonnier

CASEMATE
Philadelphia & Oxford

Contents

Introduction

Whatever your motivation, collecting and renovating military vehicles or modeling, you will without doubt find this book of interest. It will readily find a place in the grubby workshop of the "Mechanic of the Impossible" or next to the paintbrushes of the most meticulous modeler.

However it is not aimed exclusively at modelers, and so also presents previously unpublished facts to the local history enthusiast, baffled by photographs taken on a summer's day in 1944, during the liberation of the village where his grandparents lived: Who is this American unit with lined-up Jeeps and Dodges along a high street decorated with Allied flags?

It also provides all the details needed by the collector who wants to make the final touches to the vehicle he has restored with so much care: the markings are authentic and coherent.

As soon as the choice of the vehicle—the most representative of which are illustrated throughout these pages—has been made, the only thing left to do is to define the positioning of the national markings and the units that you want to represent, as long as the vehicle was ineed part of its table of equipment. This is, in fact, the main focus of this book. Each chapter includes a detailed and generously illustrated explanatory section. We have compiled a volume of accessible information that will allow the aficionado to make credible representations. Careful observation of the equipment displayed in museums or at association meetings have shown us that this is not always the case—this book will help you ensure your representation is correct.

Jean Bouchery, 2017

Below.
Army maneuvers in Montana in the 1930s, with peacetime markings clearly visible. These 1½-ton Dodge trucks, 4x2 (1934 model) carry on their doors the fully spelled-out 4th Infantry Regiment, Service Company, and the insignia of the 3rd Division. (P. Charbonnier Collection)

3

ARSENAL OF DEMOCRACY

1

In this chapter we look at the United States during World War II and summarize data on the production of military matériel and its diversity.

The Neutrality Act was passed on November 4, 1939, repealing laws that forbade the export of war equipment. Freedom to reinstitute exports was granted to private enterprises, provided that the clients pay cash, with the producer being responsible for the delivery of the goods: the Cash and Carry clause. At that time in the war, this measure exclusively benefited France and Great Britain, the powers of the Axis having practically no way of resorting to it.

On March 11, 1941, while the U.S. was still neutral, President Roosevelt obtained from Congress approval for the Lend-Lease Act, which allowed to give, lend or rent any material, service or information destined to a nation whose actions were considered by the president as vital for the defense of the United States.

Compensation could be made as payments, return of the goods or any other direct or indirect advantage that the president deemed satisfactory.

LEND-LEASE DELIVERIES	
USSR	
Medium Tank M4A2	4,102
Halftrack	1,156
Light Tank M3/M5	1,386
Jeep	49,250
2½-ton Truck, Studebaker 6x6/6x4	190,000
Great Britain	
Medium Tank M4A1, A2, A4	15,246
Halftrack	5,690
Light Tank M5/M5A1	1,650
M10 Tank Destroyer	1,648
Jeep	104,430
France	
Medium Tank M4	750
Halftrack	1,431
Light Tank M3/M5	226
M10 Tank Destroyer	255
75mm Howitzer Motor Carriage	174
M8 Light Armored Car	400
M20 Utility Armored Car	160
Jeep	9,500

The strength of the American economy is demonstrated in this photograph, taken at an armored vehicle park in Great Britain before the D-Day landings. Note the added armor soldered over the original white star marking.

Above.
Taken from a commemorative leaflet from the Chrysler Society, these images show the assembly lines of its Dodge subsidiary.

Even before the U.S. officially entered the conflict, such measures allowed its industry to prepare for war.

Left.
May 3, 1945, Grabow, Germany. A Sherman M4A2 (76) from the Red Army. In order to standardize the Soviets asked for diesel-engine tanks, as in their models of national construction.
(National Archives)

Scooter, Motor, 2-wheel, Airborne

Technical Manual TM 9-876
Parts list SNL G-683
Manufacturer: Cushman Motor Works
Use: parachutable motorcycle
Allocation: airborne units

Motorcycle, solo

Technical Manual TM 10-1177/10-1359/10-361/
10-1175/10-1331 (Harley-Davidson), TM 10-1279
(Indian)
Parts list SNL G-523 (HD), G)524 (Indian)
Manufacturer: Harley-Davidson Motor Co. Model
WLA (photo), Indian Motorcycle Co. Model 640-B.
Use: dispatch transport, reconnaissance troops
and military police

Car, Medium Sedan 5-passenger, 4x2

Technical Manual TM 10-1303/10-1133
(Chevrolet), TM 10-1375 (Ford), TM 10-1149/10-
1151 (Plymouth)
Parts list SNL G-520 (Chevrolet), G-521
(Plymouth), G-522 (Ford)
Manufacturer: Chevrolet Motor Division (General
Motors Corp.), Ford Motor Co. (photo), Plymouth
Division, Chrysler Motor Corp.
Use: transport of senior officers and generals
Allocation: all unit types, divisions and above

Truck, ¼-ton, 4x4 (Jeep)

Technical Manual TM 10-1103/10-153 (Willys),
TM 10-1101/10-1349 (Ford)
Parts list SNL G-503
Manufacturer: Willys Overland Motors Co., Ford
Motor Co.
Use: personnel and light cargo transport,
reconnaissance, 37mm antitank gun tractor
Allocation: most units

Truck, Amphibian, ¼-ton, 4x4

Technical Manual TM 10-1263
Parts list SNL G-504
Manufacturer: Ford Motor Co.
Use: staff transport on land or in water
Allocation: engineers units, reconnaissance

Technical Manual TM 9-808/9-808A/9-808B
Parts list SNL G-502
Manufacturer: Dodge Brothers Corp. (Division of
Chrysler Corp.)
Use: senior officer transport on the battleground,
vehicle equipped with a radio
Allocation: most tactical units at the beginning
of the war, often replaced by the Jeep which was
more discreet at the front

Truck, Command and Reconnaissance, ¾-ton, 4x4

Truck, Weapons Carrier, ¾-ton, 4x4

Technical Manual TM 9-808/9-808A/9-808B
Parts list SNL G-502
Manufacturer: Dodge Brothers Corp. (Division of
Chrysler Corp.)
Use: tactical truck
Allocation: most units

Truck, Ambulance, ¾-ton, 4x4

Technical Manual TM 9-808/9-808A/9-808B
Parts list SNL G-502
Manufacturer: Dodge Brothers Corp. (Division of
Chrysler Corp.)
Use: transport of ill or wounded, four patients on
stretchers or eight sitting patients
Allocation: Medical Department units

Truck, Cargo and Personnel Carrier, 1½-ton, 6x6

Technical Manual TM 9-810/9-1808A
Parts list SNL G-507
Manufacturer: Dodge Brothers Corp. (Division of
Chrysler Corp.)
Use: tactical truck, for personnel and light cargo,
57mm M1 antitank gun tractor
Allocation: most tactical units

Technical Manual TM 9-901
Parts list SNL G-508
Manufacturer: General Motors Corporation
Use: transport of personnel and supplies
Allocation: most tactical units and services
Note: similar trucks by Studebaker and Reo
were mostly delivered to the USSR

Truck, Cargo, 2½-ton, 6x6

Truck, Tank, Water, 700-gal 2½-ton, 6x6

Technical Manual TM 9-801
Parts list SNL G-508
Manufacturer: General Motors Truck & Coach division of Yellow Truck and Coach Mfg. Co.
Use: drinking water transport (700 gal)
Allocation: engineer units

Truck, Dump, 2½-ton, 6x6

Technical Manual TM 10-1261
Parts list SNL G-508
Manufacturer: General Motors Truck & Coach division of Yellow Truck and Coach Mfg. Co.
Use: dumper truck for engineers / supply transport
Allocation: engineer units

Technical Manual TM 9-801 (truck), TM 5-5060 (compressor)
Parts list SNL G-508
Manufacturer:
– Frame: General Motors Truck & Coach division of Yellow Truck and Coach Mfg. Co.
– Compressor: Le Roi D318
Use: air supply for pneumatic tools
Allocation: engineer units

Truck, Air Compressor, 2½-ton, 6x6

Technical Manual TM 9-801
Parts list SNL G-138-144, 146 & 149
Manufacturer: General Motors Truck & Coach division of Yellow Truck and Coach Mfg. Co.
Use: maintenance truck in the Ordnance Department or Signal Corps. The workshop type body has various tools and machinery depending on the mission: repairs of light and heavy weaponry, instruments, mechanics, electrics, etc.

Truck, Maintenance, Ordnance, 2½-ton, 6x6

Truck, Amphibian, 2½-ton, 6x6

Technical Manual TM 9-802
Parts list SNL G-501
Manufacturer: General Motors Truck & Coach division, Yellow Truck and Coach Mfg. Co.
Use: transport on land and in water
Allocation: amphibious truck companies of the QMC (see page 46)

Technical Manual TM 10-117/10-1567/10-1569 (Autocar), TM 10-1107/10-1407/10-1459 (Federal)
Parts list SNL G-513 (Federal), G-510 (Autocar)
Manufacturer: The Autocar Co., Federal Motor Truck Co.
Use: trailer tractor
Armament: possibility to adapt an M36 mount for an AA machine gun
Allocation: Quartermaster Corps truck companies (see page 17)

Truck, Tractor, 4/5-ton, 4x4

Car, Armored, Light M8

Technical Manual TM 9-743
Parts list SNL G-136
Manufacturer: Ford Motor Co.
Use: reconnaissance
Armament: 37mm M6 gun, 1 x .30 M1919A4 machine gun, 1 x M1 rifle
Allocation: mechanized cavalry units, reconnaissance units, armored units
Crew: 4

Technical Manual TM 9-743
Parts list SNL G-176
Manufacturer: Ford Motor Co.
Use: rapid transport of personnel and cargo, command vehicle
Armament: 1 x .50 machine gun, 5 x M1 rifles, 1 x bazooka
Allocation: as for the M8 and Tank Destroyer battalions
(see page 45)
Crew: 6

Car, Armored, Utility M20

Carrier, Personnel, Halftrack M3

Technical Manual TM 9-710A/9-1710/9-1711
Parts list SNL G-102
Manufacturer: The Autocar Co., Diamond T Motor Car Co., White Motor Co.
Use: armored troop transport
Armament: 1 x .30 M1919A4 machine gun, 1 x .45 machine pistol
Allocation: armored units, armored infantry units
Crew: 12-man squad + 1 driver

Tank, Light M5

Technical Manual TM 9-732/1727
Parts list SNL G-103
Manufacturer: Cadillac Motor Car Division
(General Motors Corp.)
Use: light tank
Armament: 37mm M6 gun, 2 x .30 M1919A4
machine guns, 1 x .45 machine pistol
Allocation: tank battalions, mechanized cavalry
units (reconnaissance)
Crew: 4

Technical Manual TM 9-729
Parts list SNL G-200
Manufacturer: Cadillac Motor Car Division
(General Motors Corp.)
Use: light tank
Armament: 75mm M6 gun, 1 x .50 M2 machine
gun on the turret, 2 x .30 M1919A4 machine
guns, 4 x .45 M3 machine pistols, or 3 x PM and
1 x M1 rifle with M8 grenade launcher
Allocation: light tank battalions, mechanized
cavalry units (reconnaissance)
Crew: 5

Tank, Light M24

Tank, Medium M4

Technical Manual TM 9-371/1730
Parts list SNL G-104
Manufacturers: Baldwin Loco. Works, American
Locomotive Co., Detroit Tank Arsenal (Chrysler),
Pressed Steel Car Co., Pullman Standard Car Mfg. Co.
Use: medium tank
Armament: 75mm M3 gun, 1 x .50 M2 machine gun
on the turret, 2 x .30 M1919-A4 machine guns,
1 x .45 machine pistol, 4 x .45 pistols
Allocation: tank battalions
Crew: 5

Technical Manual TM 9-735
Parts list SNL G-226
Manufacturers: Fisher Tank Arsenal, Detroit
Tank Arsenal
Use: heavy tank
Armament: 90mm M3 gun, 1x .50 M2 machine
gun on the turret, 2 x .30 M1919A4 machine
guns, 5 x .45 M3 machine pistols, 1 x M2
carbine
Allocation: tank battalions
Crew: 5

Tank, Heavy M26

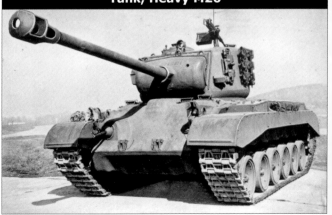

Technical Manual TM 9-738
Parts list SNL-G-185, 6, 7, 8
Manufacturers: as per M4 tank
Armament: 81mm M1 mortar, 1 x .50 M2 machine
gun on the turret, 1 x .30 M1919A4 machine gun,
1 x .45 machine pistol
Allocation: tank battalions, breakdown recovery
vehicle

Tank Recovery Vehicle M32

Carriage, Motor, 3in. gun M10

Technical Manual TM 9-752/9-1750
Parts list SNL G-130
Manufacturer: Fisher Tank Division of GM Corp.
Use: tank destroyer
Armament: 3-inch M7 gun, 1 x .50 M2 machine
gun, 5 x M1 rifles
Allocation: tank destroyer battalions
Crew: 5

Technical Manual TM 9-755
Parts list SNL G-163
Manufacturer: Buick Motor Div. of General Motors
Corp.
Use: tank destroyer
Armament: 76mm M1A1 gun, 1 x.50 M2 machine
gun, 5 x M1 rifles
Allocation: tank destroyer battalions
Crew: 5

Carriage, Motor, 76mm gun M18

Carriage, Motor, 90mm gun M36

Technical Manual 9-748
Parts list G-233
Manufacturer: Buick Motor Div. of GM Corp.
Use: tank destroyer
Armament: 90mm M3 gun, 1 x .50 M2 machine
gun, 5 x M1 rifles
Allocation: tank destroyers battalion
Crew: 5

Carriage, Motor, 75mm howitzer M8

Technical Manual TM 9-732/9-1727
Parts list SNL G-127
Manufacturer: Cadillac Motor Car Div. (GMC)
75mm self-propelled assault gun
Armament: 75mm M2/M3 howitzer, 1 x .50 M2
machine gun, 1 x .45 machine pistol, 3 x M1 rifles
Allocation: mechanized cavalry units
(reconnaissance), armored infantry, light tank
battalions
Crew: 4

Carriage, Motor, 105mm howitzer M7

Technical Manual TM 9-731/9-1750/1751
Parts list SNL G-128
Manufacturer: American Locomotive Co.
Use: self-propelled gun
Armament: 105mm M2A1 howitzer, 1 x .50 M2 machine gun, 7 x M1 rifles
Allocation: armored artillery, divisional and army/corps units
Crew: 7

Technical Manual TM 9-751/9-1750/1751
Parts list SNL G-158
Manufacturer: Pressed Steel Car Co.
Use: self-propelled gun
Armament: 155mm M1918 M1 gun, 5 x .30 rifles, 1 x grenade launcher
Allocation: army/corps heavy artillery units
Crew: 6

Carriage, Motor, 155mm gun, M12

Technical Manual TM 10-1109/10-1159/10-1553 (Corbitt), TM 10-1477/10-1601 (Mack), TM 10-1221/10-1467 (White)
Parts list: SNL G-512 (Corbitt), G-514/532 (Mack), G-547 (Brockway)
Manufacturer: Brockway Motor Co., Corbitt Co., Mack Mfg. Corp, White Motor Co. (photo)
Use: artillery tractor, engineer and ammunition transport, lowbed trailer to transport bulldozer, cranes and bridging material
Armament: option for M36 AA machine gun mounting (Mack/Corbitt)
Allocation: artillery and engineers

Truck, Prime Mover, 6-ton, 6x6

Tractor, High Speed M4

Technical Manual TM 9-7785
Parts list SNL G-150
Manufacturer: Allis-Chalmers Co.
Use: AA gun tractor (3in and 90mm) and campaign artillery (155mm gun, 8in and 240mm howitzers), personnel and ammunition transport
Armament: 1 x .50 M2 machine gun
Allocation: heavy artillery and AA battalions
Crew: 11

Technical Manual TM 9-786
Parts list SNL G-162
Manufacturer: International Harvester Co.
Use: 105 M2 and 155 M1 howitzer tractor, 4.5in gun, ammunition transport
Armament: 1 x .50 M2 machine gun
Allocation: army/corps artillery units
Crew: 9

Tractor, High Speed M5

Tractor, High Speed M6

Technical Manual TM 9-788
Parts list SNL G-1 84
Manufacturer: Allis-Chalmers Mfg. Co.
Use: 240mm howitzer and 8in gun tractor, ammunition transport
Armament: 1 x .50 M2 machine gun
Allocation: army/corps artillery units
Crew: 10

Technical Manual TM 10-1297/10-1335/10-1533/10-1605/10-1607
Parts list SNL G-509
Manufacturer: Diamond T Motor Car Co.
Use: lifting and towing of broken-down vehicles and tanks
Allocation: ordnance units and reserve

Truck, Wrecker, 4-ton 6x6

Truck, Heavy Wrecker, 10-ton, 6x6 M1

Technical Manual TM 9-795/9-1795
Parts list SNL G-116
Manufacturer: Kenworth Motor Truck Corp., Ward-LaFrance Truck Corp. (photo)
Use: lifting and towing of broken-down vehicles, tanks and machinery
Allocation: ordnance units

Truck-Trailer 45-ton, Tank Transporter M19

M20 Diamond T Truck-tractor & M9 Rogers 45-ton trailer

TM 10-1225
Parts list SNL G-159
Manufacturer: Diamond T Motor Car Co., Model 980-981
Use: transport of armor and supplies
Allocation: ordnance units

Truck-Trailer 40-ton, Tank Recovery M26

*M26 truck tractor &
M15 Fruehauf 40/45-ton trailer*

TM 9-767/9-1767
Parts list SNL G-160
Manufacturer: Pacific Car and Foundry Co.
Use: recovery and transport of armor
Allocation: ordnance units

Cargo Carrier M29

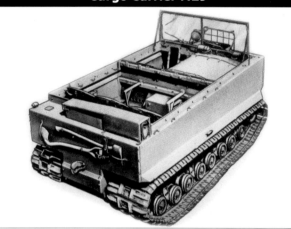

Technical Manual TM 9-772
Parts list SNL G-154
Manufacturer: The Studebaker Corp.
Use: troop transport and supply on snowy or impraticable terrain
Allocation: mountain or engineer units

Cargo Carrier M29C

TM 9-772/Parts list SNL G-179
Manufacturer: The Studebaker Corp.
Use: amphibious version of the M29 by adding watertight compartments
Allocation: engineer units

Landing Vehicle Tracked, Armored Mark II

Technical Manual TM 9-775
Parts list SNL G-168
Manufacturer: Food Machinery Corp (FMC)
Armament: 1 x .50 M2 machine gun, 2 or 3 x .30 M1919A4 machine guns
Use: troop transport in marshlands or water
Allocation: amphibian tractor battalions of the Armored force

Technical Manual TM 5-3068
Parts list SNL G-089
Manufacturer: Caterpillar Tractor Co.
Use: traction and earthwork
Allocation: engineer units
Crew: 1

Tractor, Crawler, Caterpillar D7

Trailer, Cargo, Amphibian, ¼-ton

Technical Manual TM 10-281 (American Bantam),
TM 10-1230 (Willys-Overland)
Parts list SNL G-529
Manufacturer: American Bantam Car Co., Willys-Overland Motors Inc.
Use: supply trailer on land and in water
Allocation: any unit equipped with jeeps

Trailer, 1-ton, Water Tank 250-gallon

Technical Manual TM 10-464
Parts list SNL G-527
Manufacturer: The Ben Hur Mfg. Co., The Checker
Cab Co., Springfield Auto Works
Use: trailer for drinkable water transport
(250 gal)
Allocation: all units

Trailer, Cargo, 1-ton, standard

Parts list SNL G-518
Manufacturer: American Bantam Car Co., The Ben
Hur Mfg. Co., Century Boat Works, The Checker
Cab Co. amongst others
Use: flat-bottomed trailer with wooden frame and
back dropside
Allocation: all units

Trailer, Armored, 1-ton M8

Technical Manual TM 9-761
Parts list SNL G-157
Manufacturer: John Deere Plow Works
Use: armored trailer for fuel and ammunition
transport, towed by a tank or tracked vehicle
Allocation: armored units

THE COMMUNICATIONS ZONE

2

The Communications Zone (Com Z) was the rear section of the theater of operations, adjacent to the combat zone, which accommodated lines of communication, supply and evacuation facilities, as well as the infrastructure necessary to support and maintain the combat units.

The Red Ball Express

On August 23, 1944, the Advance Section of the Com Z in France was informed of the advance beyond the Seine. Two large depots were then opened immediately behind the two advancing armies, in Dreux for the First Army, and in Chartres for the Third Army. Given the disastrous state of the French railways—destroyed by the air force in order to stop the Germans from accessing the front—82 percent of supplies, ammunition, fuel, and rations that arrived in Normandy needed to be transferred by road, starting from Saint-Lô. A one-way-route system between Normandy and the depots was reserved for these high-priority convoys, signposted with red disks on a white background. It was the birth of the famous Red Ball Express, named after an American express train service.[1]

A 4/5-ton 4X4 tractor truck produced by Autocar with a 10-ton trailer starts its journey on the Red Ball Express. The red disk sign on the grille shows it is allocated to this reserved route.
(National Archives)

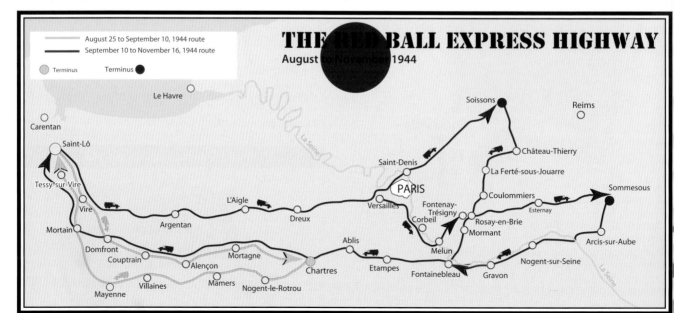

QUARTERMASTER TRUCK COMPANY

See also text box on page 19

Company Headquarters	x1	x1	x2		2½-ton truck

| | | | Weapons carrier |

| Truck Platoon (x3): | Platoon HQ | x1 | | ¼-ton truck |

| | | | 1-ton trailer |

Truck Section (x3): x8

This never-ending chain of vehicles started off on August 25, 1944, under the direction of the Transportation Corps, which controlled 132 Truck Companies—5,958 trucks—that carried on average 410,000 tons of goods every day.

It ended on November 16, 1944; by that time the circuit had developed to a total length of 1,500 kilometers, with stops in Soissons and Sommesous on the Marne, near Vitry le François. As well as Transportation Corps staff, three companies of Military Police were present in the transit towns, reinforced by an infantry regiment and the French police.

Other Express Highways

The Red Ball wound down when railways and waterways came on stream, and thanks to the access to modern ports like Antwerp. In order to ensure the prompt transit of first-necessity products (100 tons a day) to the Paris area, the Little Red Ball was put in place in December 1944 for about a month, until the railways were fixed.

In order to benefit from the ports of Le Havre and Rouen, the White Ball Express route was opened early October 1944 until January 1945, with around 30–50 truck companies.

The Green Diamond Express route was also inaugurated in October, to link the depots

---

[1] It is also thought that the Americans took inspiration from the French example of the "Voie Sacrée" that linked Bar-le-Duc to Verdun in 1916: 7,000 vehicles of all kinds traveled on this road daily, and the convoys were marked with a red disk.

Above.
These tanker trucks bear the markings of the Advance Section Com Z, 3990th Truck Company. The second truck has a gasoline sign on its grille.

Inset.
The generic insignia of the Army Service Forces, worn amongst others by the Communications Zone personnel.

A convoy of the 3886th Truck Company, Quartermaster Corps gets ready for the road. The GMC is marked as the first vehicle in the line, and the convoy commander is in the Jeep on the left. This light vehicle belonging to the HQ Company displays a low number (2).

CONVOY COMMANDER

CONVOY LEAD VEHICLE

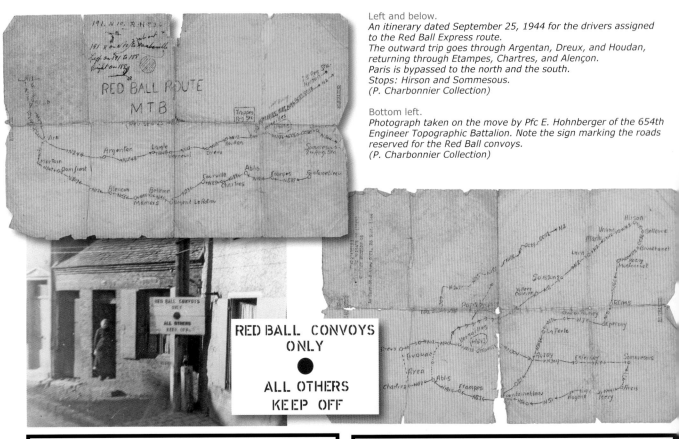

Left and below.
An itinerary dated September 25, 1944 for the drivers assigned to the Red Ball Express route.
The outward trip goes through Argentan, Dreux, and Houdan, returning through Etampes, Chartres, and Alençon.
Paris is bypassed to the north and the south.
Stops: Hirson and Sommesous.
(P. Charbonnier Collection)

Bottom left.
Photograph taken on the move by Pfc E. Hohnberger of the 654th Engineer Topographic Battalion. Note the sign marking the roads reserved for the Red Ball convoys.
(P. Charbonnier Collection)

COMMUNICATIONS ZONE, NOVEMBER 1944 TO JANUARY 1945

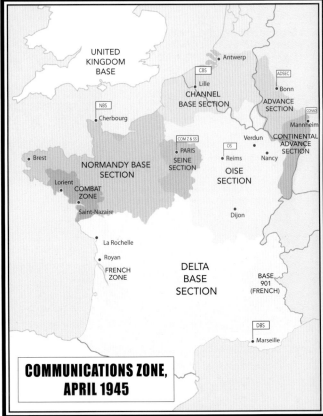

COMMUNICATIONS ZONE, APRIL 1945

Locally made and unofficial insignia of the Trucks Companies' (TC) personnel, brought under the Motor Transport Service.

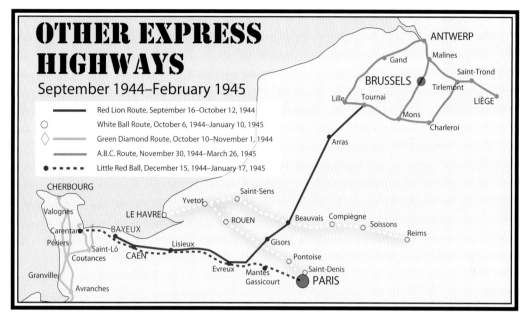

OTHER EXPRESS HIGHWAYS

September 1944–February 1945

▬▬▬	Red Lion Route, September 16–October 12, 1944
○	White Ball Route, October 6, 1944–January 10, 1945
◇	Green Diamond Route, October 10–November 1, 1944
▬▬	A.B.C. Route, November 30, 1944–March 26, 1945
●- - -	Little Red Ball, December 15, 1944–January 17, 1945

The **Quartermaster Truck Company** (see table page 17) was a separate unit that had to be able to transport any cargo (troops or supplies), at any time of day or night, to any destination as directed by the high command. It was employed independently, or within battalions, or battalion groups, and constituted a pool of vehicles and staff.

The Q.M. Truck Co. Heavy was equipped with 10-ton trailers, or tractors and fuel tankers. Its transport capacity was triple that of a standard company, which was equipped with 2½-ton trucks.
(Sources: TO&E 10-57, FM 10-35)

at the rear of the Normandy Base Section with the freight stations of Avranches and Dol-de-Bretagne. Around 15 truck companies were allocated to it, until November 1, 1944.

The Red Lion Express route was opened between September 16 and October 12, 1944, in order to transport fuel and U.S. supplies from Bayeux to the depots of the 21st British Army Group in Brussels, in preparation for the airborne operation in the Netherlands.

The A.B.C. (Antwerp–Brussels–Charleroi) Express route was put in place with a view to manage the movement of supplies in Antwerp, between the end of November 1944 and March 26, 1945. Also employed on this route were 14 companies of 10-ton trailer trucks. Around 250,000 tons were moved to the rear depots, serving the First and Ninth Armies. Shortly after the victory in Europe,

a second A.B.C. route was created in order to unblock the Antwerp and Ghent depots, thanks to 14 companies deployed from Iran.

The last great convoy route was the X.Y.Z. Express route, to support the final push into Germany. Its departure points were Liège, Düren, Luxembourg, and Nancy in order to supply depots for the Ninth, First, Third and Seventh Armies respectively. The Motor Transport Service (M.T.S.) of the Transportation Corps put in place three transport divisions that operated from March 21 to May 31, 1945. At full capacity, the X.Y.Z. route employed 244 companies, 125 of which were equipped with 10-ton trailer trucks, and 92 2½-ton standard trucks or cab-over-engine trucks. The other companies were equipped with 10-ton diesel trucks, tanker trucks, various trailers, and refrigerated trucks.

On January 23, 1945 in Belgium, a convoy on the A.B.C. route. The truck is an International M425, 4x2, 4/5-ton tractor. The unit markings on a white background are: CZ MTS 3573 QM TC TRK 32 (Com Z, Motor Transport Service, 3573rd QM Truck Company, Truck No 32). (National Archives)

3 ORGANIZATION OF THE UNITED STATES ARMY

Each unit of the U.S. Army had a fixed complement of vehicles and specific models that were allocated to its various components in a very specific way.

Indeed, whilst Jeeps, GMCs, and Dodge 4x4s were found in almost every unit and service, a good number of more specific models were reserved for certain units and missions.

In order to avoid making a mistake in the markings of a restored vehicle, for example by attributing it to a unit that did not possess such a model, it is essential to refer to the Tables of Organization and Equipment (T/O&E).

These tables indicate with precision the details and the allocation of:

- The personnel, their ranks, and roles
- The armament
- The vehicles and machines that the units were allocated

Several of these documents are presented in this chapter. They concern the armored, the infantry, and the airborne divisions, but are limited to

the subject that we are dealing with here, which are vehicles and machines. Whatever the model you might want to reproduce—an actual vehicle or a model kit—consulting these tables will help avoid mistakes commonly observed on restored vehicles: a wrecker, for example, was never allocated to an airborne division, but to an armored one. A Command Car Dodge WC56 was assigned to a division's headquarters, but not to a reconnaissance squadron.

The vehicle's employment having been determined, the only thing left is to paint on the appropriate markings of the chosen unit.

In this chapter, we will discuss which vehicles were assigned to which units that fought in Europe. Other tables will indicate the order of battle of the larger units, and the numbering of the units that constituted them.

Composition, Organization, and Numbers

The U.S. Army was made up of the fusion between the regular army and the National Guard,[1] to which were added a multitude of new units, put together for wartime deployment only. There was no independent air force in the U.S. at the time, as it was under the control of the army.

The regular army and the National Guard were brought up to their war quota, for officers principally by calling up the reserve officers, and for the rank and file by enlistment or the draft thanks to the Selective Service Training and Service Act. The length of the service was the duration of the war plus six months.

The Army

The field army was a combat force of variable structure, able to take on independent operations and comprising two army corps or more, as well as support and general reserve units. The organization of an army changed according to the needs of the operational theater in

[1] The National Guard was created in 1903, from the State militias. It was made up of reserve units, raised from each state, equipped and trained by the regular army, but which remained under the control of the State governor in time of peace. In time of war, and upon the president's order, they were included in the order of battle.

Left.
August 1943 in the USA, the crew of an M7 self-propelled gun of the 14th Armored Division is lined up for inspection. Its unit markings are partially visible on the machine-gun mounting. Note the M10 ammunition trailer attached to it.

which it was deployed. Similarly, the support units that were under its direct control were those necessary to constitute a force adequate for this theater.

The Army Corps

An army corps was a combat force of variable structure, made up of two divisions or more, with support units from the general reserve. Its supplies and transport were provided by units from the army level, apart from when the army corps operated independently. The structure of the army corps varied according to the needs of the operational theater.

The Division

The division was the smallest formation to include all the armed units and services, that allowed it to lead strategic operations on its own.

During the conflict, divisions of the following type were created with between 9,000 and 16,000 men:

- Infantry division (14,250)
- Armored division (10,900)
- Mountain division (14,900)
- Airborne division (12,900)

In the following pages are simplified tables of organization and equipment for most of the larger units and their elements, which indicate the type and number of vehicles available. Note that these tables are for the most part those valid on D-Day and do not take into consideration modifications that took place up until the end of the conflict.

A 2½-ton truck from the 13th Field Artillery Observation Battalion's Battery A, VII Army Corps, comes ashore on Utah Beach in mid-June.
(National Archives)

WC 63 Truck, Headquarters Company of the 3rd Battalion, 11th Infantry Regiment, 5th Infantry Division, during the liberation of Nemours.
(C. Routier Collection)

The Infantry Division

On August 15, 1944 on a beach near Saint-Tropez, a Jeep of the 3rd Signal Company, 3rd Infantry Division, has just disembarked a landing craft. Note the unit markings on the bumper do not conform to regulation (second illustration). Compare with another Jeep of the same unit on page 86.
(National Archives)

3-3S	S 63
3-X	3S-63

The Infantry Division

The infantry division was the basis of the army's organization in the field.

It was the essential element of the army corps—most often made up of two infantry divisions and an armored division. It was the smallest formation that comprised all ground units and services, allowing it to lead strategic operations on its own. The combat value of an infantry division depended on its capacity to coordinate its weapons and services in order to sustain the offensive during that time. During active operations, the division was reinforced with a medium tank battalion, a tank destroyer battalion and an AA artillery group, all of which were separate units.

The U.S. infantry division was "triangular." Its main combat elements were three infantry regiments, accompanied by four battalions of field artillery—three 105mm battalions and one 155mm battalion—and an engineer battalion. In addition to various services was also added a mechanized reconnaissance platoon.

The organization tables of this chapter are illustrated with examples of vehicle markings, the principles of which are explained in chapter 5.

Below.
Normandy, June 1944, a command & reconnaissance truck of the 915th Field Artillery Battalion (105mm) from the 90th Infantry Division lands on Utah Beach.

90-915F	★	A-5

VEHICLE AND EQUIPMENT ALLOCATION TABLE FOR INFANTRY DIVISIONS (JULY 1943)

	Divisonal HQ	Special troops[1]	Infantry Regiment (x3)	Divisional Artillery	Recon. Troop	Engineer Bn.	Medical Bn.	Total
Airplane, liaison				10				10
Boats, assault						14		14
Compressor, air, truck-mounted						4		4
Tractor, gas engine-driven, 35 DBHP						3		3
Trailer, lowbed, 8-ton						3		3
Trailer, utility pole type, 2½-ton						10		10
Water supply equipment, engineer						4		4
Welding equipment set #1, trailer mtd						1		1
Ambulance, ¾-ton							30	30
Car, armored, light, M8					13			13
Car, 5 passenger, sedan, medium		1						1
Halftrack M3A1					5			5
Gun, 57mm, antitank		3	18					57
Howitzer, 105mm			6	36				54
Howitzer, 155mm				12				12
Trailer, ammunition M10				60				60
Trailer, ¼-ton, cargo		1	66	46			6	251
Trailer, 1-ton, cargo		79	28	36	5	21	9	234
Trailer, 1-ton, 250-gal water							5	5
Truck, ¼-ton 4x4		64	139	82	24	16	9	612
Truck, ¾-ton, command & recon. 4x4		14		36	5		1	56
Truck, ¾-ton, weapons carrier 4x4		17	12	78		8	14	153
Truck, 1½-ton, cargo 6x6		14	30				2	106
Truck, 2½-ton, cargo 6x6		78	33	55	1	22	14	269
Truck, 2½-ton, dump						27		27
Truck, 2½-ton, small-arms repair		3						3
Truck, 2½-ton, short wheel base				84				84
Truck, 4-ton, cargo				15		3		18
Truck, 4-ton, wrecker		2		1		1		4
Truck, heavy wrecker		1						1
Trailer, K-52 (Signal Corps)		1						1

[1] See order of battle below and on page 24.
The division had very few vehicles of its own: it could be motorized by attaching six 2½-ton Quartermaster Truck Companies, see page 17.

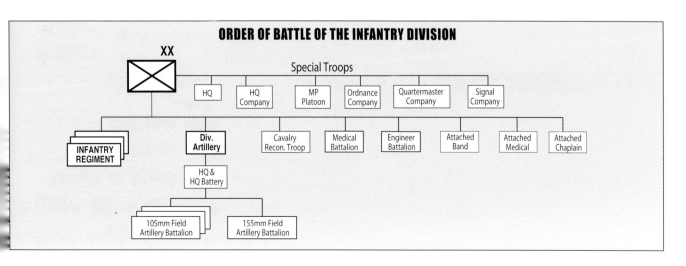

ORDER OF BATTLE OF THE INFANTRY DIVISION

XX

Special Troops

HQ — HQ Company — MP Platoon — Ordnance Company — Quartermaster Company — Signal Company

INFANTRY REGIMENT — Div. Artillery — Cavalry Recon. Troop — Medical Battalion — Engineer Battalion — Attached Band — Attached Medical — Attached Chaplain

HQ & HQ Battery

105mm Field Artillery Battalion — 155mm Field Artillery Battalion

INFANTRY DIVISION EQUIPMENT, ORGANIZATION AND MARKINGS

To present the components of the infantry division and their unit markings, we have chosen the 28th Infantry Division (more detail on page 25). The examples of markings on the side of the tables correspond to their placement at the front of the vehicles and machines.

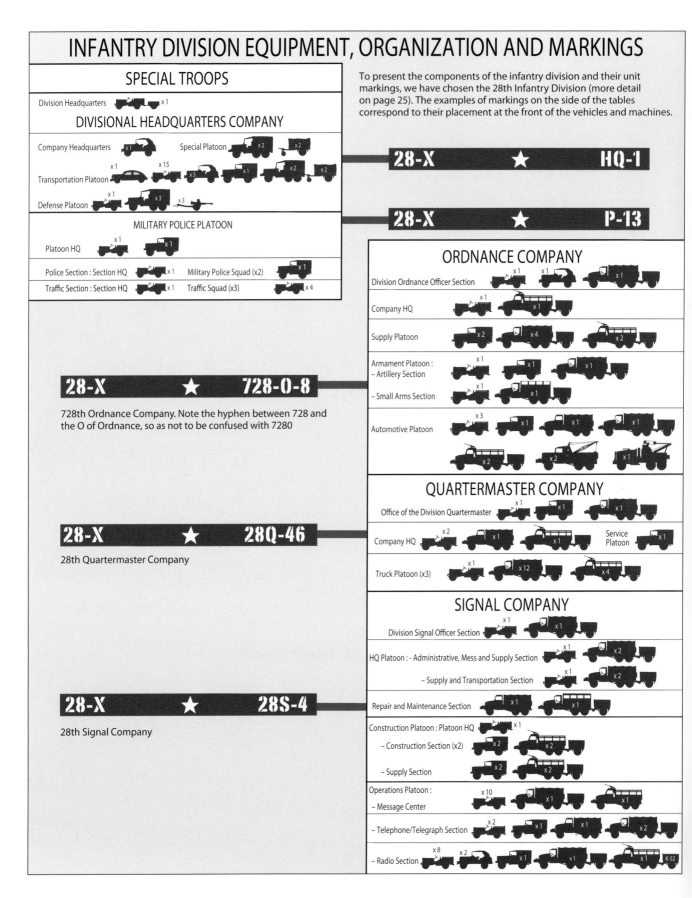

SPECIAL TROOPS

Division Headquarters x1

DIVISIONAL HEADQUARTERS COMPANY

Company Headquarters x1 — Special Platoon x2
Transportation Platoon x1 x15 x5 x1 x2 x2
Defense Platoon x1 x3 x3

28-X ★ HQ-1

28-X ★ P-13

MILITARY POLICE PLATOON

Platoon HQ x1 x1
Police Section : Section HQ x1 — Military Police Squad (x2) x1
Traffic Section : Section HQ x1 — Traffic Squad (x3) x4

28-X ★ 728-O-8

728th Ordnance Company. Note the hyphen between 728 and the O of Ordnance, so as not to be confused with 7280

28-X ★ 28Q-46

28th Quartermaster Company

28-X ★ 28S-4

28th Signal Company

ORDNANCE COMPANY

Division Ordnance Officer Section x1 x1
Company HQ x1
Supply Platoon x2 x4
Armament Platoon :
– Artillery Section x1 x1 x1
– Small Arms Section x1
Automotive Platoon x3 x1 x1
x2 x2

QUARTERMASTER COMPANY

Office of the Division Quartermaster x1
Company HQ x2 x1 — Service Platoon x1
Truck Platoon (x3) x1 x12 x4

SIGNAL COMPANY

Division Signal Officer Section x1
HQ Platoon : - Administrative, Mess and Supply Section x1
– Supply and Transportation Section x1 x2
Repair and Maintenance Section x1 x1
Construction Platoon : Platoon HQ x1
– Construction Section (x2) x2 x2
– Supply Section x2 x2
Operations Platoon :
– Message Center x10 x1 x1
– Telephone/Telegraph Section x2 x1 x1 x2
– Radio Section x8 x2 x1 x1 x1 K-52

COMPOSITION OF THE INFANTRY DIVISIONS THAT FOUGHT IN EUROPE, 1944–1945

Division	Infantry Regiments			Field Artillery Battalions				Recon. Troop	CIC Det.	Medical Bn.	Engineer Bn.	Ordnance Co.	QM Co.	Signal Co.
1	16	18	26	5	7	32	33	1	1	1	1	701	1	1
2	9	23	38	12	15	37	38	2	2	2	2	702	2	2
3	7	15	30	9	10	39	41	3	3	3	10	703	3	3
4	8	12	22	20	29	42	44	4	4	4	4	704	4	4
5	2	10	11	19	21	46	50	5	5	5	7	705	5	5
8	13	28	121	28	43	45	56	8	8	8	12	708	8	8
9	39	47	60	26	34	60	84	9	9	9	15	709	9	9
26	101	104	328	101	102	180	263	26	26	114	101	726	26	39
28	109	110	112	107	108	109	229	28	28	103	103	728	28	28
29	115	116	175	110	111	224	227	29	29	104	121	729	29	29
30	117	119	120	113	118	197	230	30	30	105	105	730	30	30
34	133	135	168	125	151	175	185	34	34	109	109	734	34	34
35	134	137	320	127	161	216	219	35	35	110	60	735	35	35
36	141	142	143	131	132	133	155	36	36	111	111	736	36	36
42	222	232	242	232	392	402	542	42	42	122	142	742	42	132
44	71	114	324	156	157	217	220	44	44	119	63	744	44	44
45	157	179	180	158	160	171	189	45	45	120	120	700	45	45
63	253	254	255	718	861	862	863	63	63	363	263	763	63	563
65	259	260	261	720	867	868	869	65	65	365	265	765	65	565
66	262	263	264	721	870	871	872	66	66	366	266	766	66	566
69	271	272	273	724	879	880	881	69	69	369	269	769	69	569
70	274	275	276	725	882	883	884	70	70	370	270	770	70	570
71	5	14	66	564	607	608	609	71	71	371	271	771	251	571
75	289	290	291	730	897	898	899	75	75	375	275	775	75	575
76	304	385	417	302	355	364	901	76	76	301	301	776	76	76
78	309	310	311	307	308	309	903	78	78	303	303	778	78	78
79	313	314	315	310	311	312	904	79	79	304	304	779	79	79
80	317	318	319	313	314	315	905	80	80	305	305	780	80	80
83	329	330	331	322	323	324	908	83	83	308	308	783	83	83
84	333	334	335	325	326	327	909	84	84	309	309	784	84	84
85	337	338	339	328	329	403	910	85	85	310	310	785	85	85
86	341	342	343	331	332	404	911	86	86	311	311	786	86	86
87	345	346	347	334	335	336	912	87	87	312	312	787	87	87
88	349	350	351	337	338	339	913	88	88	313	313	788	88	88
89	353	354	355	340	341	563	914	89	89	314	314	714	405	89
90	357	358	359	343	344	345	915	90	90	315	315	790	90	90
91	361	362	363	346	347	348	916	91	91	316	316	791	91	91
92	365	370	371	597	598	599	600	92	92	317	317	792	92	92
94	301	302	376	301	356	390	919	94	94	319	319	794	94	94
95	377	378	379	358	359	360	920	95	95	320	320	795	95	95
97	303	386	387	303	365	389	922	97	97	322	322	797	97	97
99	393	394	395	370	371	372	924	99	99	324	324	799	99	99
100	397	398	399	373	374	375	925	100	100	325	325	800	100	100
102	405	406	407	379	380	381	927	102	102	327	327	802	102	102
103	409	410	411	382	383	384	928	103	103	328	328	803	103	103
104	413	414	415	385	386	387	929	104	104	329	329	804	104	104
106	422	423	424	589	590	591	592	106	106	331	81	806	106	106

INFANTRY DIVISION EQUIPMENT, ORGANIZATION AND MARKINGS

Example of the 112th Infantry Regiment from the 28th Infantry Division. The examples of markings on the side of the tables correspond to their placement at the front of the vehicles and machines.

INFANTRY REGIMENT

HEADQUARTERS COMPANY

Company HQ

Communications Platoon

Intelligence and Recon. Platoon : Platoon HQ — Reconnaissance Squad (x2)

28-112-I ★ HQ-5

CANNON COMPANY

Company HQ

Cannon Platoon (x3) : Platoon HQ

Howitzer Section (x2)

28-112-I ★ CN-13

ANTITANK COMPANY

Company HQ

Antitank Platoon (x3) : Platoon HQ — Antitank Squad (x3)

Antitank Mine Platoon (x3) : Platoon HQ — Mine Squad (x3)

28-112-I ★ AT-16

SERVICE COMPANY

Company HQ

Regiment HQ Platoon : Supply Section

28-112-I ★ SV-31

Transportation Platoon

Platoon Headquarters — Battalion Section (x3)

Antitank Co. Section — Cannon Co. Section

HQ Co. Section — Maintenance Section

INFANTRY BATTALION (x3)

Example of the 1st Battalion of the 112th Infantry (Cos A, B, C, and D) from the 28th Infantry Division

HEADQUARTERS & HEADQUARTERS COMPANY

Battalion HQ Section

Company HQ — Ammunition & Pioneer Platoon

Communications Platoon

Antitank Platoon : Platoon HQ — Antitank Squad (x3)

28-112-I ★ 1HQ-4

RIFLE COMPANY (x3)

Weapons Platoon HQ

28-112-I ★ B-2

HEAVY WEAPONS COMPANY

Company HQ

Machine Gun Platoon (x2) : Platoon HQ — Machine Gun Squad (x2)

Mortar Platoon (x2) : Platoon HQ — Mortar Squad (x2)

28-112-I ★ D-9

The Heavy Weapons Company is the 4th in the battalion (Company D, in the 1st Battalion). Companies of the 2nd Battalion are E-F-G-H, and for the 3rd Battalion Companies I-K-L-M. The letter J was not used to avoid confusion with Company I.

INFANTRY DIVISION EQUIPMENT, ORGANIZATION AND MARKINGS

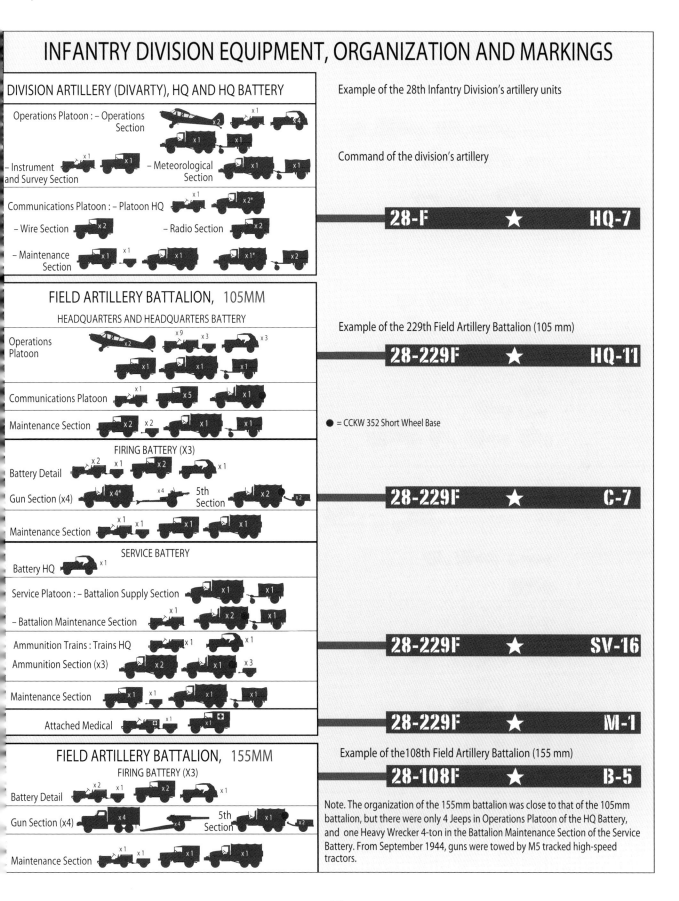

DIVISION ARTILLERY (DIVARTY), HQ AND HQ BATTERY

Operations Platoon : – Operations Section x2 x1 x4

– Instrument and Survey Section x1 x1 – Meteorological Section x1 x1

Communications Platoon : – Platoon HQ x1 x2*

– Wire Section x2 – Radio Section x2

– Maintenance Section x1 x1 x1 x1* x1

FIELD ARTILLERY BATTALION, 105MM

HEADQUARTERS AND HEADQUARTERS BATTERY

Operations Platoon x2 x9 x3 x3 x1 x1 x1

Communications Platoon x1 x5 x1

Maintenance Section x2 x2 x1 x1

FIRING BATTERY (X3)

Battery Detail x2 x1 x2 x1

Gun Section (x4) x4* x4 5th Section x2 x2

Maintenance Section x1 x1 x1 x1

SERVICE BATTERY

Battery HQ x1

Service Platoon : – Battalion Supply Section x1 x1

– Battalion Maintenance Section x1 x2 x1

Ammunition Trains : Trains HQ x1 x1

Ammunition Section (x3) x2 x3

Maintenance Section x1 x1

Attached Medical x1

FIELD ARTILLERY BATTALION, 155MM

FIRING BATTERY (X3)

Battery Detail x2 x1 x1

Gun Section (x4) x4 x4 5th Section x2

Maintenance Section x1 x1 x1 x1

Example of the 28th Infantry Division's artillery units

Command of the division's artillery

28-F ★ HQ-7

Example of the 229th Field Artillery Battalion (105 mm)

28-229F ★ HQ-11

● = CCKW 352 Short Wheel Base

28-229F ★ C-7

28-229F ★ SV-16

28-229F ★ M-1

Example of the108th Field Artillery Battalion (155 mm)

28-108F ★ B-5

Note. The organization of the 155mm battalion was close to that of the 105mm battalion, but there were only 4 Jeeps in Operations Platoon of the HQ Battery, and one Heavy Wrecker 4-ton in the Battalion Maintenance Section of the Service Battery. From September 1944, guns were towed by M5 tracked high-speed tractors.

INFANTRY DIVISION EQUIPMENT, ORGANIZATION AND MARKINGS

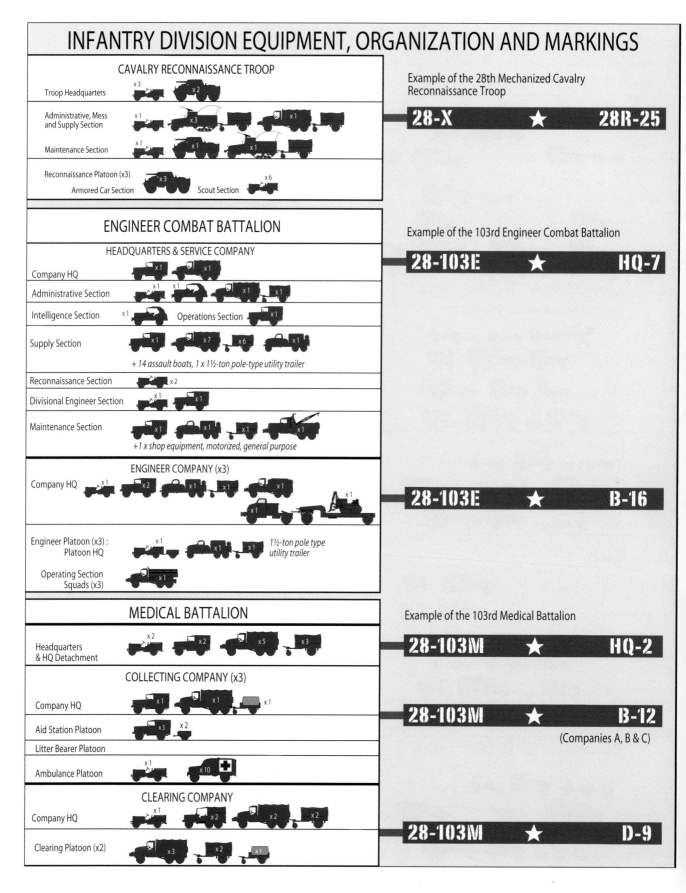

CAVALRY RECONNAISSANCE TROOP

Troop Headquarters

Administrative, Mess and Supply Section

Maintenance Section

Reconnaissance Platoon (x3)
Armored Car Section   Scout Section

Example of the 28th Mechanized Cavalry Reconnaissance Troop

28-X   ★   28R-25

ENGINEER COMBAT BATTALION

HEADQUARTERS & SERVICE COMPANY

Company HQ

Administrative Section

Intelligence Section   Operations Section

Supply Section

+ 14 assault boats, 1 x 1½-ton pole-type utility trailer

Reconnaissance Section

Divisional Engineer Section

Maintenance Section

+1 x shop equipment, motorized, general purpose

Example of the 103rd Engineer Combat Battalion

28-103E   ★   HQ-7

ENGINEER COMPANY (x3)

Company HQ

Engineer Platoon (x3) :
Platoon HQ   *1½-ton pole type utility trailer*

Operating Section
Squads (x3)

28-103E   ★   B-16

MEDICAL BATTALION

Headquarters & HQ Detachment

COLLECTING COMPANY (x3)

Company HQ

Aid Station Platoon

Litter Bearer Platoon

Ambulance Platoon

Example of the 103rd Medical Battalion

28-103M   ★   HQ-2

28-103M   ★   B-12

(Companies A, B & C)

CLEARING COMPANY

Company HQ

Clearing Platoon (x2)

28-103M   ★   D-9

The Armored Division

Officially created in July 1940, the Armored Force was initially just an arm of study, doctrine, and instruction.

It was halfway through 1942 that three of the first armored divisions (1st, 2nd, and 3rd) became operational with M3 medium tanks, soon followed by the new Sherman M4s. Organized as per TO&E 17 from March 1, 1942, the armored divisions were 14,620 men strong, the spearhead comprising 232 tanks organized in two regiments, supplemented by a mounted infantry regiment. During the large maneuvers and early engagements in North Africa, the number of tanks appeared too high and the infantry undermanned. The new table on September 14, 1943, brought profound modifications with the introduction of light divisions, numbers being brought down to 10,937 men and tanks being reorganized in three battalions, totaling 186 machines. For various reasons, the 2nd and 3rd Armored Divisions retained the heavy configuration of 1942.

In combat, the division was organized into combat commands (A, B and R for reserve), with, depending on tactical needs, a tank battalion, a self-propelled artillery battalion, an engineer detachment, and so on.

On campaign, the armored division played a role of in-depth penetration and exploitation due to its mobility and its firepower, scouts being provided by a squadron of mechanized cavalry.

Right.
Germany 1945. The table on page 31, which indicates that the 43rd Tank Battalion belonged to the 12th Armored Division, allows us to identify this Sherman despite the fact that the 1 of the 12th Armored has been erased at the front of this tank, leaving us to think it might be the 2nd Armored Division.
(National Archives)

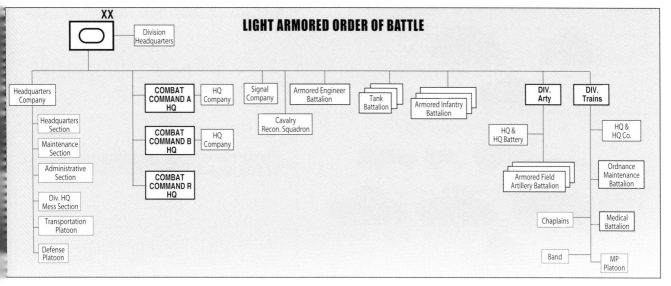

LIGHT ARMORED ORDER OF BATTLE

ARMORED DIVISION EQUIPMENT, ORGANIZATION AND MARKINGS

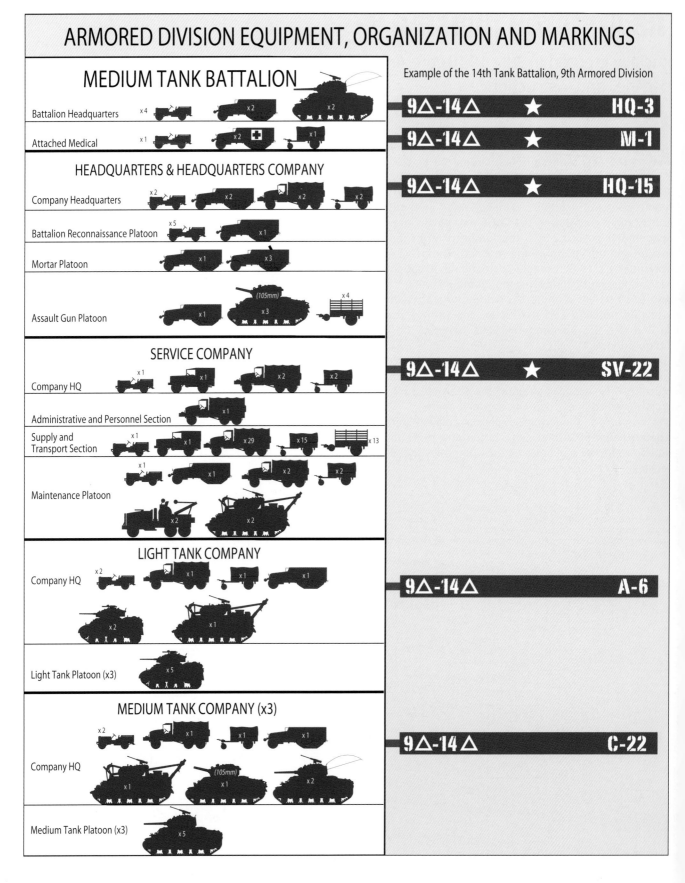

MEDIUM TANK BATTALION

Battalion Headquarters — x 4, x 2, x 2

Attached Medical — x 1, x 2, x 1

HEADQUARTERS & HEADQUARTERS COMPANY

Company Headquarters — x 2, x 2, x 1, x 2

Battalion Reconnaissance Platoon — x 5, x 1

Mortar Platoon — x 1, x 3

Assault Gun Platoon — x 1, (105mm) x 3, x 4

SERVICE COMPANY

Company HQ — x 1, x 1, x 2, x 2

Administrative and Personnel Section — x 1

Supply and Transport Section — x 1, x 1, x 29, x 15, x 13

Maintenance Platoon — x 1, x 1, x 2, x 2, x 2, x 1

LIGHT TANK COMPANY

Company HQ — x 2, x 1, x 1, x 1, x 2, x 1

Light Tank Platoon (x3) — x 5

MEDIUM TANK COMPANY (x3)

Company HQ — x 2, x 1, x 1, x 1, x 1, (105mm) x 1, x 2

Medium Tank Platoon (x3) — x 5

Example of the 14th Tank Battalion, 9th Armored Division

9△-14△ ★ HQ-3

9△-14△ ★ M-1

9△-14△ ★ HQ-15

9△-14△ ★ SV-22

9△-14△ A-6

9△-14△ C-22

EQUIPMENT TABLE OF THE ARMORED DIVISION'S[1] MAIN COMPONENTS (FEBRUARY 1944)

	Div HQ	CCA HQ	CCB HQ	CCR HQ	Signal Co.	Cav. Rcn. Sqn.	Tank Bn. x3	AIB x3	Div. Arty	Engineer Bn.	Div. trains[2]	Total
Airplane, liaison									8			8
Compressor, air, truck mounted										4		4
Tractor crawler, 35 DBHP										3		3
Trailer, lowbed, 8-ton										3		3
Trailer, utility 2½-ton Type I										9		9
Truck, cargo, treadway, 6-ton										6		6
Water supply equipment, engineer										4		4
Welding equipment, trailer mounted										1		1
Truck, surgical											6	6
Ambulance, ¾-ton											30	30
Car, armored, light, M8	2					52						54
Car, armored, utility M20									1			1
Car, 5-passenger, medium sedan											1	1
Car, halftrack	12	7	7		19	32	13	72	90	15	11	448
Carriage, motor, 75mm howitzer						8		3				17
Carriage, motor, 105mm howitzer									54			54
Carrier, 81mm mortar, halftrack M21							3	3				18
Gun, 57mm, antitank	3							9				30
Tank, light,	3	3	3			20	18					83
Tank, medium							53	9				168
Tank, medium, w. 105mm howitzer							6					18
Trailer, ammunition, M10		1	1			14	17	8	99	2		192
Trailer, ¼-ton, cargo		2	2						5		3	12
Trailer, 1-ton, cargo	3	2	2		10	34	26	21	64	24	92	372
Trailer, 1-ton, 250-gal water											6	6
Truck, ¼-ton, Jeep[3]	9	9	9		22	106	22	23	69	25	67	451[3]
Truck ¾-ton, command & recon.							1	1	6	1	14	27
Truck ¾-ton, weapons carrier	2						1	1	14	6	33	61
Truck, 2½-ton, artillery repair											3	3
Truck, 2½-ton, automotive repair											6	6
Truck, 2½-ton, cargo	3	2	2		19	20	39	21	80	27	93	426
Truck, 2½-ton, dump										18		18
Truck, 2½-ton, electrical repair											3	3
Truck, 2½-ton, instrument repair											3	3
Truck, 2½-ton, machine shop											7	7
Truck, 2½-ton, small arms repair											3	5
Truck, 2½-ton, welding											4	4
Truck, 4-ton, cargo											3	3
Truck, heavy wrecker										1	11	25
Truck, trailer, 40-ton, tank recovery[4]										9	9	
Vehicle, tank recovery, M32							5	1	6			24
Trailer, K-52					6							6

Abbreviations:
CCA HQ: Combat Command A HQ; Cav. Rcn Sqn: Cavalry Reconnaissance Squadron; Tk Bn: Tank Battalion; AIB: Armored Infantry Battalion; Div. Arty: Divisional Artillery
[1] Apart from the 2nd and 3rd Armored Divisions, which were classified as heavy divisions with tank and infantry regiments and a reconnaissance battalion.
[2] Division trains encompass Quartermaster, Ordnance, and Military Police.
[3] Including Ford GPA amphibious Jeeps usually allocated to the Engineer Battalion.
[4] Progressively replaced by the M26 Pacific, also found in separate ordnance units.

Note: Not mentioned, solo motorcycles were issued to the divisional and battalion headquarters, along with 25 halftrack ambulances of the medical battalion.

ARMORED DIVISION EQUIPMENT, ORGANIZATION AND MARKINGS

ARMORED INFANTRY BATTALION

Example of the 52nd Armored Infantry Battalion, one of three such units of the 9th Armored Division

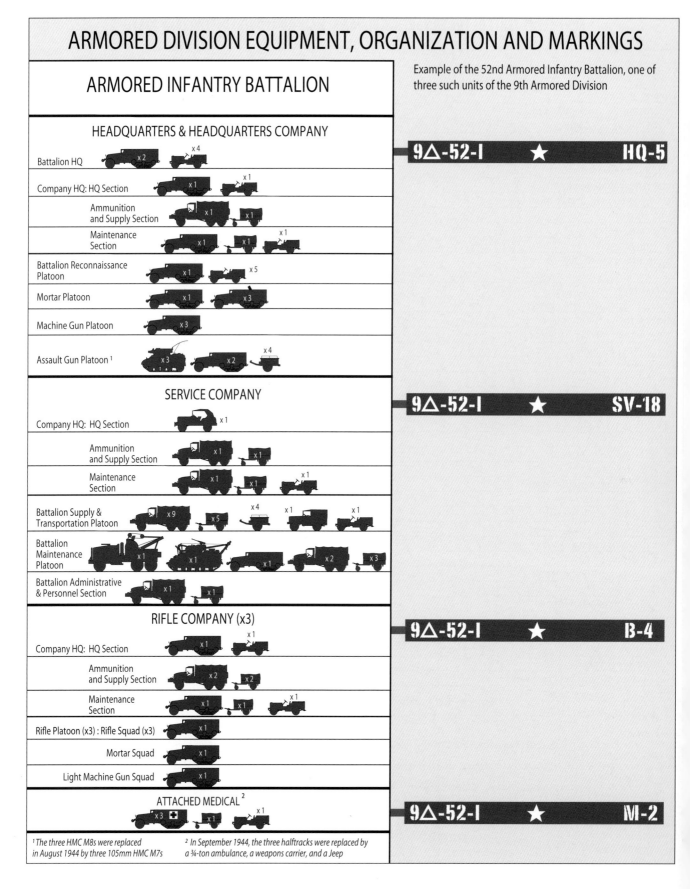

HEADQUARTERS & HEADQUARTERS COMPANY

Battalion HQ — x 2, x 4

Company HQ: HQ Section — x 1, x 1

Ammunition and Supply Section — x 1, x 1

Maintenance Section — x 1, x 1, x 1

Battalion Reconnaissance Platoon — x 1, x 5

Mortar Platoon — x 1, x 3

Machine Gun Platoon — x 3

Assault Gun Platoon [1] — x 3, x 2, x 4

9△-52-I   ★   HQ-5

SERVICE COMPANY

Company HQ: HQ Section — x 1

Ammunition and Supply Section — x 1, x 1

Maintenance Section — x 1, x 1, x 1

Battalion Supply & Transportation Platoon — x 9, x 5, x 4, x 1, x 1

Battalion Maintenance Platoon — x 1, x 1, x 2, x 3

Battalion Administrative & Personnel Section — x 1, x 1

9△-52-I   ★   SV-18

RIFLE COMPANY (x3)

Company HQ: HQ Section — x 1, x 1

Ammunition and Supply Section — x 2, x 2

Maintenance Section — x 1, x 1, x 1

Rifle Platoon (x3) : Rifle Squad (x3) — x 1

Mortar Squad — x 1

Light Machine Gun Squad — x 1

9△-52-I   ★   B-4

ATTACHED MEDICAL [2]

x 3, x 1

9△-52-I   ★   M-2

[1] The three HMC M8s were replaced in August 1944 by three 105mm HMC M7s

[2] In September 1944, the three halftracks were replaced by a ¾-ton ambulance, a weapons carrier, and a Jeep

32

ARMORED DIVISION EQUIPMENT, ORGANIZATION AND MARKINGS

ARMORED FIELD ARTILLERY BATTALION
(Table for November 1944)

Example of the 73rd Armored Field Artillery Battalion, one of three such units of the 9th Armored Division

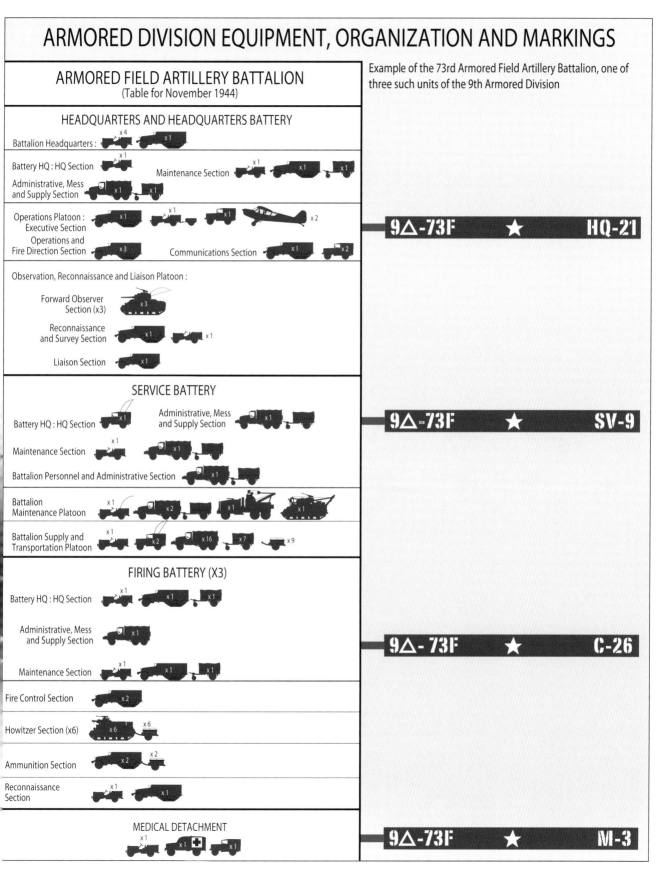

HEADQUARTERS AND HEADQUARTERS BATTERY

Battalion Headquarters :

Battery HQ : HQ Section

Maintenance Section

Administrative, Mess and Supply Section

Operations Platoon : Executive Section

Operations and Fire Direction Section

Communications Section

Observation, Reconnaissance and Liaison Platoon :

Forward Observer Section (x3)

Reconnaissance and Survey Section

Liaison Section

9△-73F ★ HQ-21

SERVICE BATTERY

Battery HQ : HQ Section

Administrative, Mess and Supply Section

Maintenance Section

Battalion Personnel and Administrative Section

Battalion Maintenance Platoon

Battalion Supply and Transportation Platoon

9△-73F ★ SV-9

FIRING BATTERY (X3)

Battery HQ : HQ Section

Administrative, Mess and Supply Section

Maintenance Section

Fire Control Section

Howitzer Section (x6)

Ammunition Section

Reconnaissance Section

9△- 73F ★ C-26

MEDICAL DETACHMENT

9△-73F ★ M-3

COMPOSITION OF THE ARMORED DIVISIONS THAT FOUGHT IN EUROPE, 1944–1945

Division	Tank Battalion/ Armored Regiment			Armored Infantry Battalion/ Regiment			Armored Field Artillery Battalion			Rcn Sqn./ Bn.	CIC Det.[4]	Armd. Medical Bn.	Armd. Eng. Bn.	Armd. Ordnance Bn.	Armd. Signal Bn.
1[1]	1	4	13	6	11	14	27	68	91	81	501	47	16	123	141
2	66[2]	67[2]	-	41[2]	-	-	14	78	92	82[3]	502	48	17	2	142
3	32[2]	33[2]	-	36[2]	-	-	54	67	391	83[3]	503	45	23	3	143
4	8	35	37	10	51	53	22	66	94	25	504	4	24	126	144
5	10	34	81	15	46	47	47	71	95	85	505	75	22	127	145
6	15	68	69	9	44	50	128	212	231	86	506	76	25	128	146
7	17	31	40	23	38	48	434	440	489	87	507	77	33	129	147
8	18	36	80	7	49	58	398	399	405	88	508	78	53	130	148
9	2	14	19	27	52	60	316	73	89		509	2	9	131	149
10	3	11	21	20	54	61	419	420	423	90	510	80	55	132	150
11	22	41	42	21	55	63	490	491	492	41	511	81	56	133	151
12	23	43	714	17	56	66	493	494	495	92	512	82	119	134	152
13	24	45	46	16	59	67	496	497	498	93	513	83	124	135	153
14	25	47	48	19	62	68	499	500	501	94	514	84	125	136	154
16	5	16	26	18	64	69	393	396	397	23	516	216	216	137	156
20	9	20	27	8	65	70	412	413	414	30	520	220	220	138	160

[1] In 1944–1945, the 1st Armored Division only fought in Italy.
[2] These units are actual regiments as the 2nd and 3rd Armored Divisions had not been restructured as light divisions by September 1943.
[3] Armored Reconnaissance Battalion.
[4] Counter Intelligence Corps Detachment. For interrogation of prisoners of war and suspicious civilians.

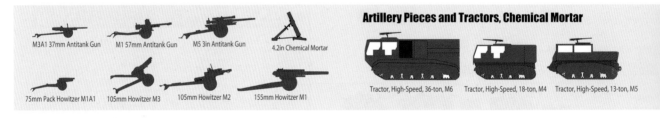

M3A1 37mm Antitank Gun — M1 57mm Antitank Gun — M5 3in Antitank Gun — 4.2in Chemical Mortar

75mm Pack Howitzer M1A1 — 105mm Howitzer M3 — 105mm Howitzer M2 — 155mm Howitzer M1

Artillery Pieces and Tractors, Chemical Mortar

Tractor, High-Speed, 36-ton, M6 — Tractor, High-Speed, 18-ton, M4 — Tractor, High-Speed, 13-ton, M5

Below.
Photo taken in 1942, showing the vehicles and machines of the HQ and Reconnaissance Companies of the 46th Tank Regiment, 13th Armored Division, still structured on the heavy model. Note the unit markings. The numbers 13 and 46 followed by a triangle identify the division and regiment, the letters HQ and the number are those of the sub-unit and the individual number. These markings are explained in detail in chapter 5. By 1944, the scout car and the 37mm gun on the weapons carrier on the right, were no longer allocated to U.S. armored divisions in operational theaters.
(National Archives via Jon Gawne)

Key to Organization and Equipment Tables

Motorcycle, solo, Harley-Davidson WLA

Scooter, Motor, Airborne

Car, Medium Sedan 4x2

Truck, ¼-ton, 4x4

Truck, ¼-ton, 4x4, Amphibian

Truck, ¾-ton, Command & Recon

Truck, ¾-ton 4x4 Weapons Carrier

Truck, ¾-ton 4x4 Ambulance

Truck, Cargo and Personnel Carrier 1½-ton, 6x6

Carrier, Cargo M29

Tractor, 5/6-ton, 4x4 (Mack Engineers)

Truck, Cargo, 2½-ton 6x6

Truck, Ordnance Maintenance, 2½-ton 6x6

Truck, Cargo, 2½-ton 6x6 (short wheel base)

Truck, Dump, 2½-ton 6x6

Truck Air Compressor, 2½-ton 6x6

Truck, 2½-ton 6x6 Amphibian (DUKW)

Truck, 4-ton, 6x6 (Diamond T)

6x6 4-ton Wrecker Truck Diamond T

Diesel Engine Tractor (Bulldozer)

20-ton Lowbed Semi-Trailer

Truck, 6-ton, 6x6 (Brockway)

Truck, Prime Mover, 6-ton, 6x6 (Mack Artillery)

Truck, Heavy Wrecking, 10-ton M1

M32 Armored Recovery Vehicle

M8 Armored Car, Light

M20 Armored Car, Utility

M3 Halftrack

Truck Mounted Crane M2

81mm Mortar Carrier

M15A1 Gun Motor Carriage

M16 Gun Motor Carriage

M4 Medium Tank

(105 mm)

Medium Tank 105mm Howitzer

M10 Gun Motor Carriage (3in)

M7 Howitzer Motor Carriage (105mm)

M5 Light Tank

M8 Howitzer Motor Carriage (75mm)

Trailers

Trailer, Ammunition M10

Trailer, 1-ton, Ammunition

Trailer, 1-ton, Cargo

Trailer, 1-ton, Water Tank

Trailer, ¼-ton, Cargo

L4 Observation Plane

Note: illustrations are not to scale.

To help with reading the equipment tables in this chapter, it is advised to photocopy this page spread to use as a reference.

The Airborne Division

The birth of the airborne force commenced in July 1940, at Fort Benning, Georgia, where an experimental paratrooper battalion was established.

In 1941, after promising results, an initial unit was established, the 501st Parachute Infantry Battalion, comprising 500 officers and enlisted men. Several paratrooper infantry regiments, exclusively composed of volunteers, were then set up, all numbered in the 500 series. In 1942, the 82nd Airborne Division, comprising one glider-borne regiment and two paratrooper regiments, saw action in the Mediterranean theater. The 101st and 17th Airborne Divisions would follow, which would also take part in the liberation of Europe.

In June 1944, given the increase in carrier planes, the division was brought up to a strength of 7,500 men, comprising three paratrooper regiments, and a glider regiment with two battalions, accompanied by the indispensible support and service units.

The primary mission of the airborne division was to capture various objectives by surprise, causing disarray in the enemy's rear, and to consolidate

Above, left.
July 1943, boarding for Sicily. This Jeep emplaning a Waco glider bears the markings of the 320th Glider Field Artillery Battalion, 82nd Airborne (A/B) Division, Battery A, 8th vehicle.

Above, right.
Typical of the airborne formations, the Cushman Scooter was mostly allocated to the headquarters company of a paratrooper regiment.

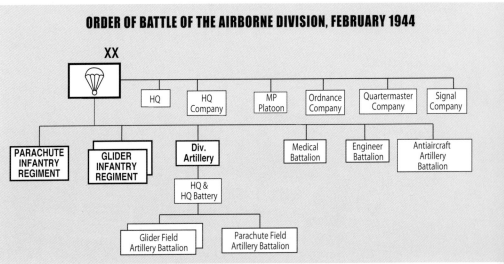

ORDER OF BATTLE OF THE AIRBORNE DIVISION, FEBRUARY 1944

established positions while waiting for ground elements to join them within the shortest period of time.

Because of these missions and their mode of transport to the battlefield, the airborne division only had minimal organic means of transport, mostly Jeeps and a large number of hand carts.

AIRBORNE DIVISION EQUIPMENT TABLE, VEHICLES AND MACHINES (FEBRUARY 1944)

	Div. HQ	Div. HQ Co.	MP Platoon	Divisional Artillery	PIR	GIR (x2)	AEB	QM Co.	Signal Co.	Medical Co.	A/B AAA Bn.	Ordnance Co.	Total
Car, 5-passenger, sedan	1			1									2
Cart, hand, M3A4					27	72	20				42		233
Cart, hand, M6A1				20									20
Compressor, air, trailer mount							2						2
Gun, 57mm antitank				4		8					24		44
Howitzer, 75mm, pack				36									36
Motorcycle, solo		2											2
Scooter, motor	4			46	52	29	20	4		4	15	2	205
Servicycle[1]									9				9
Tractor, crawler type, DBHP						4							4
Trailer, dump, ½-ton						10							10
Trailer, ¼-ton		1	4	35	10	12	8	30	4	20	44	15	195
Trailer, 1-ton, cargo					13	1	27	16	16	4	2	5	87
Truck, ¼-ton (Jeep)[2]		9	4	97	15	20	19	30	4	23	44	15	300
Truck, ¾-ton, ambulance										2			2
Truck, ¾-ton, weapons carrier		5		8	1	1					2		18
Truck, 2½-ton		10		27	16	10	4						20

Abbreviations
Div. HQ: Divisional HQ
HQ Co.: Headquarters Company
MP Platoon: Military Police Platoon
PIR: Parachute Infantry Regiment

GIR: Glider Infantry Regiment
AEB: Airborne Engineer Battalion
QM Co.: Quartermaster Company
A/B AAA Bn.: Airborne Antiaircraft Artillery Battalion

Notes:
[1] The Simplex Servicycle is a small motorcycle of low displacement with two-stroke engine
[2] To the Jeeps total, add 7 Jeeps and ¼-ton trailers for the chaplains, as well as 16 Jeeps and 13 ¼-ton trailers for additional medical personnel.

AIRBORNE DIVISIONS COMPOSITION, EUROPE 1944–1945

Airborne Division	GIR	PIR	GFAB	PFAB	AAABn	Parachute Maintenance Co.	AEB	Medical Company	Signal Company	Ordnance Company	Quarter-master Co.
17th[1]	194	507 513	680 681	464 466	155	17	139	224	517	717	411
82nd[2]	I&II/325 III/401	505 507 508	319 320	456	80	-	307	307	82	782	407
101st[2]	I&II/327 I/401	501 502 506	321 907	377	81	-	326	326	101	801	426
1st ABTF[3]	550[4]	517 1/551[5]	602[6]	460 463		-	596[7]	676	512		344

[1] The units indicated for the 17th A/B Division are those assigned to the Rhine crossing in March 1945.
[2] The units indicated for the 82nd and 101st are those for Normandy in June 1944.
[3] First Airborne Task Force, created for the landings in Provence.
[4] Airborne Infantry Battalion (Glider)
[5] Parachute Infantry Battalion
[6] Field Artillery Battalion (75 Pack)
[7] Airborne Engineer Company
Abbreviations:
GFAB: Glider Field Artillery Battalion
PFAB: Parachute Field Artillery Battalion

AIRBORNE DIVISION EQUIPMENT, ORGANIZATION AND MARKINGS

PARACHUTE INFANTRY REGIMENT

Examples for the 507th Parachute Infantry Regiment of the 82nd Airborne Division, motorized vehicles only.
In the case of airborne scooters, the units markings are for guidance only; any precision would be welcome as to their placement on the vehicle.

HEADQUARTERS COMPANY

Operations Section	x 2
Intelligence Section	x 4
Communications Platoon HQ	x 4
Demolition Platoon HQ	x 4

82 A/B-507-I   HQ-10

SERVICE COMPANY

| Regiment HQ Platoon | x 2 |

| Transportation Platoon | x 15   x 10   x 1 |
| | x 16   x 16 |

82 A/B-507-I   ★   SV-9

PARACHUTE INFANTRY BATTALION (x3)

HQ Company :
    Company Headquarters :
        Headquarters Platoon x 12

82 A/B-507-I   3HQ-4

507th PIR, 3rd Battalion, HQ Company, 4th vehicle. Only the HQ company of the battalion was equipped with vehicles: 12 scooters

---

Examples for the 401st Glider Infantry Regiment of the 101st Airborne Division, motorized vehicles only.

101 A/B-401-I   HQ-3

101 A/B-401-I   ★   SV-31

GLIDER INFANTRY REGIMENT

HEADQUARTERS COMPANY

| Company Headquarters | x 29 |

SERVICE COMPANY

Company Headquarters	x 1 x 1
Regimental HQ Platoon : Staff Section	x 2
Transportation Platoon : Battalion Section (x2)	x 5 x 4
Regimental HQ Section	x 3 x 2
Heavy Section	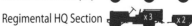 x 10 x 10
Maintenance Section	 x 1 x 1
	x 1

GLIDER INFANTRY BATTALION (x2)

Note.
In June 1944, the glider infantry battalion had in theory no motorized vehicles.

AIRBORNE DIVISION EQUIPMENT, ORGANIZATION AND MARKINGS

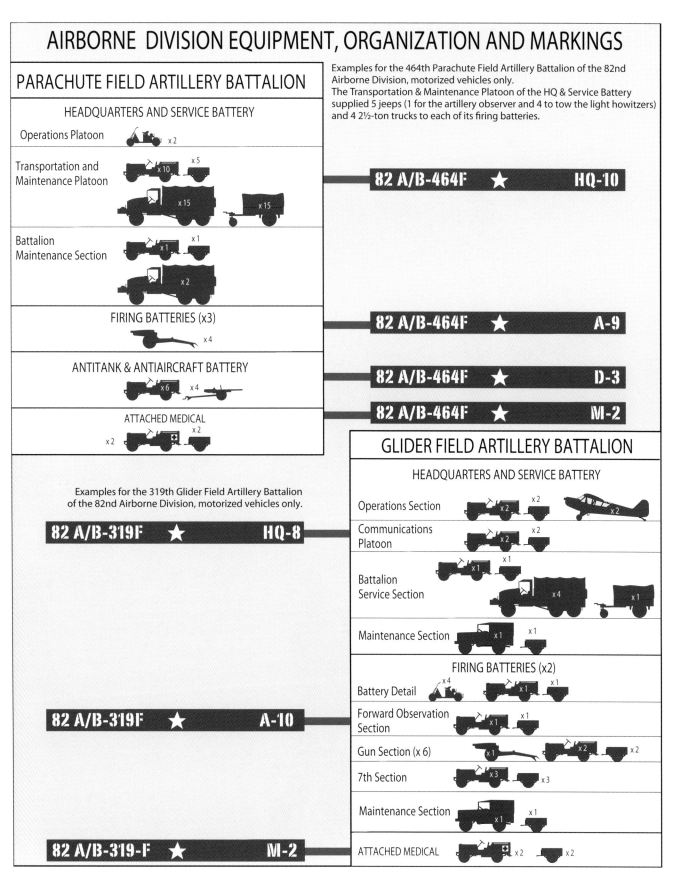

PARACHUTE FIELD ARTILLERY BATTALION

Examples for the 464th Parachute Field Artillery Battalion of the 82nd Airborne Division, motorized vehicles only.

The Transportation & Maintenance Platoon of the HQ & Service Battery supplied 5 jeeps (1 for the artillery observer and 4 to tow the light howitzers) and 4 2½-ton trucks to each of its firing batteries.

HEADQUARTERS AND SERVICE BATTERY

Operations Platoon x 2

Transportation and Maintenance Platoon x 10 x 5 x 15 x 15

Battalion Maintenance Section x 1 x 1 x 2

82 A/B-464F ★ HQ-10

FIRING BATTERIES (x3)
x 4

82 A/B-464F ★ A-9

ANTITANK & ANTIAIRCRAFT BATTERY
x 6 x 4

82 A/B-464F ★ D-3

ATTACHED MEDICAL
x 2 x 2

82 A/B-464F ★ M-2

Examples for the 319th Glider Field Artillery Battalion of the 82nd Airborne Division, motorized vehicles only.

82 A/B-319F ★ HQ-8

82 A/B-319F ★ A-10

82 A/B-319-F ★ M-2

GLIDER FIELD ARTILLERY BATTALION

HEADQUARTERS AND SERVICE BATTERY

Operations Section x 2 x 2 x 2

Communications Platoon x 2 x 2

Battalion Service Section x 1 x 1 x 4 x 1

Maintenance Section x 1 x 1

FIRING BATTERIES (x2)

Battery Detail x 4 x 1 x 1

Forward Observation Section x 1 x 1

Gun Section (x 6) x 1 x 2 x 2

7th Section x 3 x 3

Maintenance Section x 1 x 1

ATTACHED MEDICAL x 2 x 2

Non-Divisional Units
Mechanized Cavalry Groups

1A-113C   C-1

Non-divisional units were combat and service units that were not attached to a specific division, kept at the disposal of the army commander, for assignments of variable length. Depending on the needs and operations, they could range from army group to divisional level.

Non-divisional units were, for instance, tank destroyer battalions, independent tank battalions, field artillery groups, field artillery battalions (heavy), antiaircraft artillery battalions and any other support unit: engineers, medical, quartermaster, signals, ordnance, chemical warfare, etc.

In the case of the cavalry, each army corps or army fielded of a cavalry group with one HQ troop and two mechanized cavalry reconnaissance squadrons, whose basic equipment was composed of M8 armored cars, light tanks, halftracks and Jeeps.

These groups were used as scouts, flank protection, and sometimes in defense. However, their primary objective was to inform high command of the enemy's movements and his combat potential.

1A-24CR F6

Above.
September 8, 1944, at the border between the Netherlands and Germany, an M8 armored car of the 113th Cavalry Reconnaissance Squadron's Troop C. Non-divisional reconnaissance units were identified in their markings by the C for Cavalry.
(National Archives)

Left.
Light M5 tank of the 24th Cavalry Reconnaissance Squadron in training in Britain before D-Day. At the time the squadron was a non-divisional unit under the control of the First Army (1A). Here, the unit type is identified by the initials CR (Cavalry Reconnaissance, F was the Light Tank Company.
(Nicolas Conreur Collection)

VI-117 RA27

IA 4CR   C-16

Above.
August 19, 1944. During the operations of Task Force Butler in Haute-Provence, a Jeep from 117th Cavalry Reconnaissance Squadron's Troop A enters Saint-Auban.
(Guy Reymond Collection)

Above right, and right.
Liberation of Spa (Belgium), September 9, 1944. Seen here are two Jeeps of the 4th Cavalry Reconnaissance Squadron. The first is the 16th vehicle of Troop C. The First Army is indicated by a Roman I as the number 1 was unavailable in the stencils. The second Jeep is the 31st vehicle of Troop C.
(Nicolas Conreur Collection)

Below.
Another Jeep from the same unit, in Riez, a day earlier. Note the different disposition of the unit markings on the bumper. The 117th belonged to VI Corps, whose round insignia is visible on the driver's sleeve.
(Guy Reymond Collection)

VI-117R   B2

CAVALRY GROUPS COMPOSITION

Cavalry Group	Composition
2nd Cavalry Group	2nd, 42nd Cavalry Rcn. Sqn.
3rd Cavalry Group	3rd, 43rd Cavalry Rcn. Sqn.
4th Cavalry Group	4th, 24th Cavalry Rcn. Sqn.
6th Cavalry Group	6th, 28th Cavalry Rcn. Sqn.
11th Cavalry Group	11th, 38th Cavalry Rcn. Sqn.
14th Cavalry Group	18th, 32th Cavalry Rcn. Sqn.
15th Cavalry Group	15th, 17th Cavalry Rcn. Sqn.
16th Cavalry Group	16th, 19th Cavalry Rcn. Sqn.
101st Cavalry Group	101st, 116th Cavalry Rcn. Sqn.
102th Cavalry Group	102nd, 38th Cavalry Rcn. Sqn.
106th Cavalry Group	106th, 121st Cavalry Rcn. Sqn.
113th Cavalry Group	113th, 125th Cavalry Rcn. Sqn.
115th Cavalry Group	115th, 104th, 107th Cavalry Rcn. Sqn.
117th Cavalry Group	

CAVALRY RECONNAISSANCE SQUADRON, MECHANIZED (INDEPENDENT) EQUIPMENT, ORGANIZATION AND MARKINGS

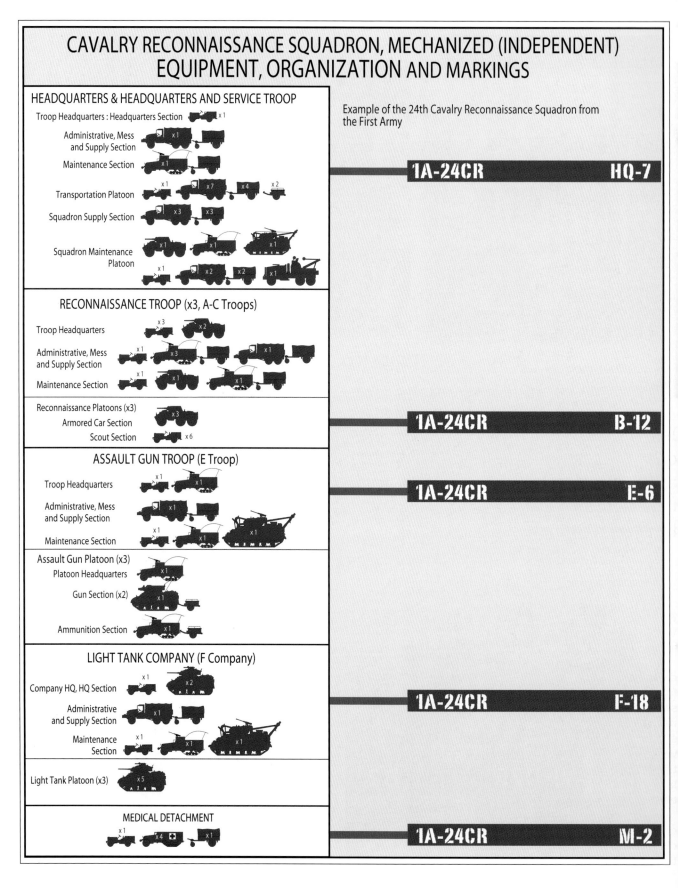

HEADQUARTERS & HEADQUARTERS AND SERVICE TROOP

Troop Headquarters : Headquarters Section — x 1

Administrative, Mess and Supply Section — x 1

Maintenance Section — x 1

Transportation Platoon — x 1 · x 7 · x 4 · x 2

Squadron Supply Section — x 3 · x 3

Squadron Maintenance Platoon — x 1 · x 1 · x 1 · x 2 · x 2

RECONNAISSANCE TROOP (x3, A-C Troops)

Troop Headquarters — x 3 · x 2

Administrative, Mess and Supply Section — x 1 · x 3

Maintenance Section — x 1

Reconnaissance Platoons (x3)
Armored Car Section — x 3
Scout Section — x 6

ASSAULT GUN TROOP (E Troop)

Troop Headquarters — x 1 · x 1

Administrative, Mess and Supply Section — x 1

Maintenance Section — x 1

Assault Gun Platoon (x3)
Platoon Headquarters — x 1
Gun Section (x2)
Ammunition Section — x 1

LIGHT TANK COMPANY (F Company)

Company HQ, HQ Section — x 1 · x 2

Administrative and Supply Section — x 1

Maintenance Section — x 1

Light Tank Platoon (x3) — x 5

MEDICAL DETACHMENT

x 1 · x 4 · x 1

Example of the 24th Cavalry Reconnaissance Squadron from the First Army

1A-24CR — **HQ-7**

1A-24CR — **B-12**

1A-24CR — **E-6**

1A-24CR — **F-18**

1A-24CR — **M-2**

Tank Battalions and Tank Destroyer Battalions

1944 Italy, seen here is an M4 Sherman medium tank of the 751st Tank Battalion, non-divisional unit of the Fifth Army, Company A's 5th machine.

5A-751△   **A-5**

In the earlier years of the conflict, during strategic assessment on the setting up of armored units, it was decided that as well as the divisions inspired by the German model, non-divisional[1] tank battalions should be created, whose main purpose would be infantry support.

Antitank operations properly speaking, were designated to be undertaken by the tank destroyer battalions, equipped in 1944–45 with towed or self-propelled pieces, positioned in ambushes in front of enemy breakthroughs.

In fact, throughout the war, infantry divisions were accompanied—sometimes for extended periods of time—by one or several tank battalions, depending on the needs. They would also be supported by self-propelled tank destroyer battalions, which were not generally fully utilized due to German panzers operating individually or in a smaller units. They proved especially useful in the assault of fortified positions.

Remember that these battalions were only supplementing infantry divisions, and did not belong to them; their machines therefore bore similar markings to those of other non-divisional units, starting most commonly with the army number.

---

[1] As of 1943, the organization of non-divisional tank battalions was identical to that of a standard divisional battalion (see page 30).

This M-10 Gun Motor Carriage, armed with a 3in antitank piece, is supporting the infantry during the fight for Aix-la-Chapelle (Aachen). These markings are these of the 634th Tank Destroyer Battalion, a First Army unit. Note that on both machines the company's letter is missing on the right.
(National Archives)

1A 634TD   **14**

43

NON-DIVISIONAL TANK BATTALIONS, EUROPE 1944–1945

46th	740th	758th (Light,
70th[1]	741st[1]	Colored)[4]
191st[3]	743rd[1]	759th
701st	744th	760th[4]
702nd	745th	761st (Colored)
707th	746th	771th
709th	747th	772nd
712th	748th	774th
714th	749th	777th
717th	751st[4]	778th
735th	752nd[4]	781st
736th[2]	753rd[3]	782nd
737th	755th[4]	784th (Colored)
738th	756th[3]	786th
739th	757th[4]	787th

Note: The battalions numbered 1st to 5th, 8th to 11th, 13th to 27th, 31st to 32nd, 34th to 37th, 40th to 41st, 43rd, 45th, 47th to 48th, 68th to 69th, 80th and 81st, belonged to divisions (see page 34)

Duplex Drive amphibious tanks:
[1] Normandy,
[2] Rhine crossing
[3] Provence
[4] Italy

TANK DESTROYER BATTALIONS (SELF-PROPELLED), EUROPE 1944–1945

601st[1]	654th[1]	806th
602nd (M18)	656th (M18/36)	808th (M36,
603rd (M18)	661st (M18)	1945)
605th (1945)	691st (M36)	809th (M18/36)
607th[1]	692nd	811th (M18)
609th (M18)	701st[2]	813th[1]
610th (M36)	702nd[1]	814th[1]
612th (M18)	703rd[1]	817th (M18)
628th[1]	704th (M18)	818th[1]
629th	705th	820th (M18)
630th (M36)	771st[1]	821st
631st	773rd[1]	822nd (M18)
633rd (M18)	774th (M36)	823rd
634th	776th[1]	824th (M18)
635th	786th[1]	825th
636th	801st (M18,	827th (M18)[3]
638th (M18)	1945)	893rd
643rd (M18)	802nd (1945)	894th[2]
644th	803rd[1]	899th[1]
645th[1]	804th[2]	

[1] Units equipped with M10 tank destroyer that received M36s in the course of the campaign (fall–winter 1944)
[2] Italy only
[3] Black units

The Ordnance Depot (ammunitions) O-609 of Soissons belonged to the Oise Intermediate Section (OIS—see map page 18) of the Communications Zone. The vehicles belong to the fire fighters of the 166th Ordnance Battalion. In between them are two dozer tanks, one of which is equipped with a high-pressure hose on the turret. (National Archives via J. Gawne)

TANK DESTROYERS EQUIPMENT, ORGANIZATION AND MARKINGS

TANK DESTROYER BATTALION (towed)
HEADQUARTERS & HEADQUARTERS COMPANY

Company HQ — x 1   x 2   Reconnaissance Platoon (x2) — x 5

Communications Platoon — x 2   x 1

Staff Platoon : Administrative Section — x 1   x 1

Intelligence and Operations Section — x 3   x 4   Supply Section — x 1

Maintenance Platoon — x 2   x 1   x 2

Transportation Platoon — x 2   x 10   x 4

GUN COMPANY (x3)

Company HQ : HQ Section — x 2   x 2   Maintenance Section — x 1   x 1

Destroyer Platoon (x3): Platoon HQ and Security Section — x 4   x 1   x 1

Destroyer Section (x2) — x 2   x 2

TANK DESTROYER BATTALION (self-propelled)
HEADQUARTERS & HEADQUARTERS COMPANY

Company HQ : HQ Section — x 1   x 1   Motor Maintenance Section — x 1

Communications Platoon — x 2   x 2

Staff Platoon : Administrative Section — x 1   x 1   Intelligence Section — x 3   x 3

Supply Section — x 1   x 1   x 1

Maintenance Platoon — x 3   Transportation Platoon — x 14   x 14

RECONNAISSANCE COMPANY

Company HQ : HQ Section — x 2   x 2   x 1   Motor Maintenance Section — x 1

Pioneer Platoon : Platoon HQ — x 1   x 1   Pioneer Section (x2) — x 2

TANK DESTROYER COMPANY (x3)

Company HQ : HQ Section — x 2   x 2

Motor Maintenance Section — x 1   x 1   x 1

Tank Destroyer Platoon (x3) Platoon HQ — x 2   x 1   x 1

Gun Section (x2) — x 2

Not illustrated for both types of battalions is the Medical Detachment, equipped with four Jeeps, a 1½-ton 6x6 truck and a 1-ton cargo trailer.

12AG-825TD ★ **HQ-4**

12th Army Group, 825th Tank Destroyer Battalion, HQ & HQ Company, 4th vehicle (June 1944)

VII-607TD ★ **B-20**

VII Corps, 607th Tank Destroyer Battalion, B Company, 20th vehicle (Note: the unit received self-propelled guns in November 1944)

XX-818TD ★ **HQ-5**

XX Corps, 818th Tank Destroyer Battalion, HQ & HQ Company, 5th vehicle

XX-818TD ★ **R-7**

XX Corps, 818th Tank Destroyer Battalion, Reconnaissance Company, 7th vehicle

1st Army, 703rd Tank Destroyer Battalion, B Company, 21st machine (M10 Gun Motor Carriage)

1A-703TD **B-21**

Other Non-Divisional Support Units

ANTIAIRCRAFT ARTILLERY BATTALION, AUTOMATIC WEAPONS, MOBILE

HQ & HQ BATTERY

 x12 x4 x9 x9

AUTOMATIC WEAPONS BATTERY (x4)

Headquarters Section x1

Communication Section x1 x1

Maintenance Section x2 x2

Auto Weapons Platoon (x2) :

Platoon Headquarters x1 x1

Firing Section (x4) : Auto Weapons Squad x1 M15A1

Machine Gun Squad x1 M16

AMPHIBIAN TRUCK COMPANY

Company HQ  x1 x2

Maintenance Platoon x1 x1 x1

Amphibian Truck Platoon (x2) :
– Platoon HQ x1

– Truck Section (x3) x8

CHEMICAL MORTAR BATTALION

HQ & HEADQUARTERS COMPANY[1]

Company HQ Section  x6 x5

Battalion HQ Section x3

Ammunition Section (x3) x14 x13

Maintenance Section

MORTAR COMPANY (x3)

Company HQ x2 x1 x2

Platoons (x3) :

Platoon HQ x2 x1

Squad (x4) x1 M29 x1

Note. For D-Day, the Jeep was replaced by a Studebaker M29 Weasel

---

Note. Organization and equipment table from November 1944; before this date, the Automatic Weapons Squad was armed with 40mm automatic guns.

3A-448 AAA AW ⭐ **A28**

Above.
A 2½-ton truck with an M51 trailer armed with quadruple .50 gun enters Janville (Eure-et-Loir) in August 1944. The unit is the 448th AAA (AW) Battalion of the Third Army, attached to the 35th Infantry Division (see markings above).
(C. Routier Collection)

6ESB   460 AM

6th Engineer Special Brigade, 460th QM Amphibian Truck Company

A halftrack from the 443rd AAA (AW) Battalion, Task Force Butler in Provence, August 1944.
(G. Reymond Collection)

[1] This is the total allocation of vehicles. Despite our research, we have been unable to find the exact allocation of the Chemical Mortar Battalion's HQ & HQ Co. Any information would be welcome.

VII-92G ⭐ **B-11**

VII Corps, 92nd Chemical Mortar Battalion, B Company, 11th vehicle

The Military Police

In the combat zones, at the front could be found the Military Police (MP) platoon from the infantry division, under the command of a divisional provost marshal. The section performed its duties between the division's rear sector and the front line, essentially taking care of road traffic, and orienting stragglers and isolated units. Its organization is detailed on page 24. The MP platoon of the armored division was identical; however, a halftrack was added to the Platoon HQ as well as four traffic squads, and for the airborne division's platoon, two Jeeps and four motorcycles to the Platoon HQ.

Farther back from the front was a platoon of Military Police ensuring army corps security led by the corps' provost marshal.

At field army level, was the Military Police Battalion, Army (T/O 19-36). Its task was to control the zone situated between the divisions and the army's rear sector. Comprised of three companies rather than four, it juxtaposed itself to an army controlling three corps. A company was added for each additional corps if necessary.

Farther still from the army zone, was the Communications Zone. The Military Police's standard battalions in charge of monitoring it were under the control of the operational theater's high command. The main difference with the army corps-level MP battalion was the addition of old-style scout cars.

(Taken from the article by Jonathan Gawne, in Militaria Magazine *no. 333)*

Jeep from an unidentified MP unit in France.

FIELD ARMY MILITARY POLICE BATTALION

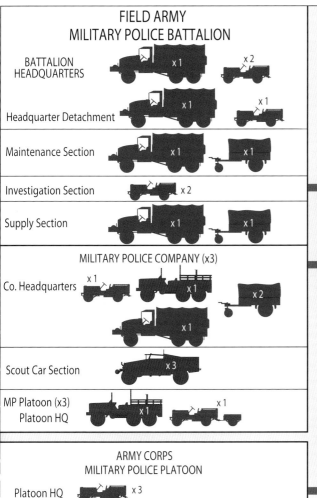

Note: Though it was not officially part of its inventory, the WLA motorbike was often present in most MP units at that time, like the divisional platoon, for example.

3A-503P ★ **HQ-8**

3rd Army, 503rd MP Battalion, Headquarters, 8th vehicle

1A-509P ★ **B-7**

1st Army, 509th MP Battalion, B Company, 7th vehicle

In 1944–45, the M3 Scout Car was no longer allocated to the U.S. Army in Europe apart from MP battalions at army level.

VII-X ★ **P-3**

VII Corps MP Platoon, 3rd vehicle

COMMON MARKINGS

Registration

M8 light armored cars of the 28th Reconnaissance Troop, 28th Infantry Division, during the parade in Paris, August 29, 1944. The registration number painted on the side of the vehicle, includes the 60 prefix for armored cars, followed by the production order number: 32837.

The Army Regulations (A.R.) AR 850-5, from August 5, 1942, defined the markings that were to go on vehicles and equipment.

The addendum to AR 850-10 on November 3, 1942, stated that all motorized vehicles had to be registered by the Motor Vehicle Central Records Office of the War Department, managed by the Chief of Ordnance, at the Tank and Automotive Center in Detroit, Michigan.

The AR 850-5 specified that the registration markings should be painted by the manufacturer at the factory, and should never be modified or painted over, even in the case of a transfer from one unit to another.

In 1942, the markings were painted in a matt blue color, then following a directive in January 1944 from the U.S. Command in Great Britain, in white.

The registration number started with W (for War Department) until January 1942.

The number, preceded, followed or topped with the initials U.S. or U.S.A., included a prefix of one or two digits, relating to the vehicle's category (see table at right). The

THE X PREFIX

The X prefix denoted a replacement registration number given to vehicles that had been completely rebuilt or fundamentally modified (like long-frame Jeeps), or those bought abroad, captured or returned by the nations that had benefited from the Lend-Lease agreement. Examples on pages 50 and 72.

MATRICULATION NUMBER PREFIX BY VEHICLE CATEGORY	
0	Trailers
00	Workshop or recovery vehicles
1	Sedans
10	Kitchen trucks
2	Vehicles under a ton*
20	Liaison and reconnaissance vehicles, buses
3	Trucks, up to 1½-tons*
30	Tanks
4	Trucks 2½ to 4/5 tons*
40	Tracked or halftrack machines (not tanks)
5	Over 5 tons* trucks, artillery tractors
50	Emergency and fire vehicles
6	Motorbike, solo
60	Armored cars and special vehicles (HQ, radio, projector)
7	Ambulances
70	Amphibious vehicles
8	Wheeled tractors
80	Tanker trucks
9	Tracked or halftrack tractors
*fully laden	

Left.
Generals Eisenhower and Bradley, North Africa, 1943. The Jeep's registration is painted matt blue, whilst the emplacement for the Suppressed S is empty.

Middle.
Halftracks lined up at a depot in Great Britain. The registration numbers (prefix 40 for halftracks) have been repainted white. The white stars on the hoods (without circle) have been covered in mud. The clover-like motif was painted in vesicant-agent-detection yellow.

Bottom.
Registration stencilling on a Dodge truck in a factory.

Registration Examples

Character heights: motorbikes, 2 inches (5cm); other vehicles and trailers, 4 inches (10cm)
(Note from HQ ETO, March 15, 1944)

From 1942 to January 1944: matt blue paint	U.S.A. 12345678
Motorcycle	U.S.A. 627327
¼-ton Truck (Jeep)	U.S.A. 20329531-S
¾-ton Truck, Command & Reconnaissance	U.S.A. 20291391-S
¾-ton Truck, Ambulance	U.S.A. 722264
2½-ton Truck	U.S.A. 4144063- S
Halftrack	U.S.A. 40571442-S
M8 Armored Car	U.S.A. 6033442-S
M4 Medium Tank	U.S.A. 3066192
M5 Light Tank	U.S.A. 3047456-S
M26 Truck, Tractor	U.S.A. 536532

DUKW from a unit of the 1st Engineer Special Brigade during an exercise before D-Day. Note the registration with the 70 prefix before the star, denoting the amphibious category, as well as the S of the radio interference suppressor. Also note the 9 bridge classification under the windshield on the left.

rest of the number was the production order number.

The markings were placed on the sides of the vehicle so as to be visible, as well as at the back if possible, but always without hindering the legibility of the unit markings.

On the vehicles having been fitted with a radio interference suppressor, the registration was followed by an S (Suppressed) and a hyphen (AR 850-5 addendum, January 27, 1944).

Above.
Non-regulation placement of markings on the motorcycle's tank. The 6 prefix is that of motorcycles. The X identifies a machine that has been re-registered, see page 48.

Left.
Detail of a 1-ton cargo trailer registration; the 0 is the prefix for this kind of equipment.
(National Archives)

Below.
Placement of the registration on a WLA motorcycle of the 2nd Armored Division in Normandy.
(National Archives)

Above.
The registration of a Jeep's trailer, from the 29th Infantry Division, painted in the old matt blue color; the star is missing. The T is probably the initial for Trailer, with a numbering typical of the equipment in this unit.

Right.
A self-propelled M7 in England before June 6. The registration starts with 40 for tracked matériel other than tanks

REGISTRATION PLACEMENT
(ILLUSTRATIONS ARE NOT TO SCALE)

U.S.A.613540

Airborne Scooter

1941–1945

February 1945

Motorcycle, solo

Sedan

U.S.A. 12843

¼-ton Truck

¼-ton Trailer

Weapons Carrier

2½-ton Truck

Halftrack

Medium Tank

Armored Car

CZCBS·3888QM(TC)·TRK·8

Left.
On this International 5-ton 4x2 truck, the registration 5108372 (prefix 5 for trucks of this weight) has been painted over the first markings.

Inset.
The unit markings in black on white (to help legibility in the Rear zone) on the bumper.
– CZ: Communications Zone
– CBS: Continental Base Section
– 3888 QM (TC), TRK-8: 3888th Quartermaster Truck Company, 8th vehicle.

Below.
This shot taken in England in June 1944 shows us the detail of the markings of the 741st Tank Battalion, which supported the 1st Infantry Division on Omaha Beach, with M4 and M4A1 tanks, equipped with wading equipment, enabling them to drive in a certain depth of water:
* *registration (prefix 30 for tanks) on the side;*
* *size and weight markings on the additional armor plate;*
* *the flag stuck to the hull front to show the waterproofing of the machine.*
On the M8 armored trailer:
* *the star painted on top;*
* *the registration on the side;*
* *the tactical markings on the front and the yellow disc from the bridge classification. These two markings are shown on the inset: 1A for First Army, the battalion being one of its general reserve units.*

National Identification Markings

Right.
In 1944–45, the star painted on upper surfaces was most often circled in white, as on the hood of this Jeep.
(Brigham Young U.)

Below.
Examples of stars for horizontal surfaces. The gaps between the star and the circle could be painted with a yellow paint that reacted to vesicant gas (circular of February 1943), by turning red (see example of a halftrack, page 61).

Also specified in the AR 850-5 of August 5, 1942, these markings were represented by a five-pointed star, such as appears on the American flag.

It was imperative that these markings figure on all vehicles and machines—whatever their model—assigned to tactical units, but also to those operating at the rear of the operational theaters.

The size of the national markings varied according to the space available on each vehicle, which often showed several stars, whose emplacements are shown in the illustrations in this chapter. Ambulances were a specific case and are dealt with separately.

When some operations necessitated their concealment, the stars could be, by command order, covered with Olive Drab paint, camouflage nets, or a mixture of grease and soil.

The white stars were often inside a large white circle, fragmented or not, the purpose being that they could be easily seen from the air. The campaigns of Western Europe would prove the necessity of this disposition, because Allied tactical aviation occasionally attacked its own troops.

In 1943, the American white star markings would be extended to all the Allied armies, and therefore shown on British, French, and Canadian machines.

Circular No. 15 HQ ETO USA, on February 16, 1943, specified that the star visible by the vehicle's driver should have the space between the points and the circle painted with dull yellow M5 paint, a vesicant agent

(Continued on page 57)

MOTORCYCLE, SOLO

Top, left.
France, July 1944, near Saint-Lô. A policeman of the 507th Military Police Battalion keeps an eye on traffic. Note the white star on the tank, as per regulation.

CAR, LIGHT SEDAN, 5-PASSENGER

NATIONAL STAR PLACEMENT

The color illustrations in this chapter are based on those of the 1942 regulations. Note that during the period mostly covered in this book, the star painted on the main surface was often within a circle (see page 53).

Depending on the vehicle, the diameter of the imaginary circle containing the star is indicated with a red letter. The table below shows these dimensions with their equivalent in inches and centimeters.

1 inch = 2.54 cm

Circle reference	Inches	Centimeters
A	4 inches	10.1 cm
B	6 inches	15.2 cm
C	10 inches	25.2 cm
D	12 inches	30.4 cm
E	15 inches	38.1 cm
F	16 inches	40.6 cm
G	20 inches	50.8 cm
H	25 inches	63.5 cm
I	32 inches	81.2 cm
J	36 inches	91.4 cm
K	40 inches	101.1 cm
L	60 inches	152.4 cm

Left.
After the end of the war in Europe, General Patton poses by his Cadillac. The plate carrying the stars of his rank is affixed at the back. The large white star fits in a circle of 38cm diameter.

TRUCK, ¼-TON, 4 X 4

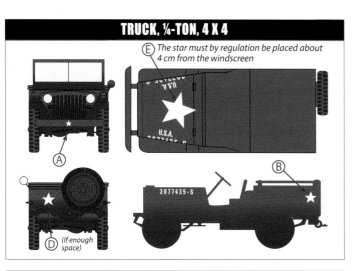

(E) The star must by regulation be placed about 4 cm from the windscreen

U.S.A.

U.S.A.

(A)

(D) (If enough space)

2077435-S

(B)

THE PAINT USED ON VEHICLES

The AR 850-15 from September 29, 1939, article 10, prescribed that all self-propelled vehicles should be painted in the regulatory Olive Drab green, apart from fire-fighting vehicles (engineers), which should be Fire Department Red and the vehicles of the Air Corps operating on airfields, which should be Chromium Yellow.

TRUCK, AMPHIBIAN, ¼-TON, 4X4

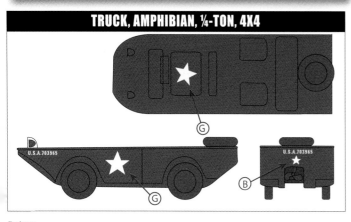

(G)

U.S.A.703965

U.S.A.703965

(G)

(B)

Below.
In training back home, is an amphibious Jeep from the 353rd Infantry, 89th Infantry Division. The star on the hull side does not comply with regulations (see above), but is identical to that of a Jeep.

Right.
Near Saint-Lô in July 1944. In order to avoid reflection, the windshield of this Jeep is covered in a canvas sheet made in situ. It still bears the identifying circled white star. In the middle of the road is a halftrack ambulance from an armored division.

Above.
Italy, 1945. A small-scale circled star at the back of this Jeep from the 92nd Infantry Division. The national markings were painted by the units, which explains the diversity in the dimensions and the methods of painting.

Below.
Thanksgiving, November 1943 in Italy. These G.I.s of the 3rd Division are enjoying a traditional turkey on the hood of their Jeep. Note the different size of the star compared to the one on page 53.

TRUCK, ¾-TON, 4X4, COMMAND & RECONNAISSANCE

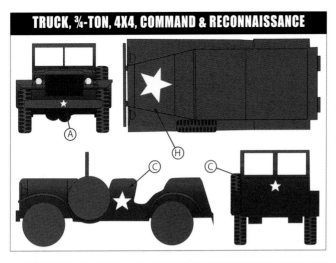

TRUCK, ¾-TON, 4X4, WEAPONS CARRIER

Note: In the case of the model with a winch, the space is insufficient for a star on the bumper

Below.
Placement of the stars on this weapons carrier of the 693rd Tank Destroyer Battalion.

Above.
In Rambervillers at the end of 1944, seen here are stars painted on the hood and bumper of a weapons carrier. The tactical markings have been smudged out.

Below.
Argentan, August 1944. A star painted on the body of a 1½-ton 6x6. In its infantry configuration, this truck tows a 57mm antitank piece.

Below.
The star on the body of this command & reconnaissance truck from 1st Engineer Special Brigade on Utah Beach. The registration number starts with 20, which makes it a liaison and reconnaissance vehicle.

TRUCK, CARGO 1½-TON, 4X4

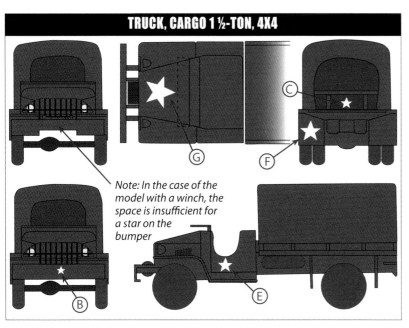

Note: In the case of the model with a winch, the space is insufficient for a star on the bumper

detector. If there was no star in the driver's field of vision, an irregular shape of at least 46cm was to be painted in this color.

Given the wide range of the U.S. Army's vehicular equipment (see Chapter 1), we present here only a selection of these vehicles, the ones most used by the units at the front as well as by those in the staging zones to the rear.

The table on page 54 shows the diameter of the imaginary circle that contained the star. These were normally painted as the vehicle came out of the factory, with large stencils, but also after revisions or repairs in the workshops, which explains the varying dimensions and placements that can be observed in contemporary photographs.

Note that the illustrations are not to scale and do not constitute a precise view of the vehicles.

Left.
Loading of a 2½-ton truck at a port in Normandy, 1944. The tactical markings on the bumper are illustrated in color in the inset, from left to right:
Black 7: bridge classification
3394 TC TRK 24: 3394th Truck Company (from the Quartermaster Corps), vehicle no. 24. The (O) signifies the unit carries Ordnance supplies.
(National Archives)

Below.
Placement of the stars on another 2½-ton truck in Normandy. Note also the sign on the grille indicating the load (Explosives, whilst in truth it is a light L-4 observation aircraft) and the unit serial number with the colored stripes code on the left of the bumper (see chapter 5).
It is probably a service battery truck from an artillery battalion.
(National Archives)

Truck, Cargo 2½-ton, 6x6, closed cab

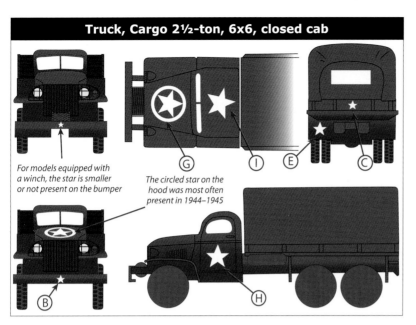

For models equipped with a winch, the star is smaller or not present on the bumper

The circled star on the hood was most often present in 1944–1945

G

I

E

C

B

H

Truck, Cargo 2½-ton, 6X6, open cab

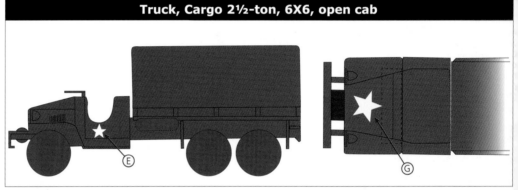

Below.
September 1944 on the Red Ball Express Highway, a convoy takes a break to swap drivers, refuel and briefly service the vehicles. The tactical markings on the bumper of the truck on the right are shown in the inset, from left to right: 4006 TC TRK 6: 4006th Truck Company, vehicle no. 6. Note the small star in the middle above the gap for the winch on the bumper.

E

G

ASCZ 4006 ★ TC TRK 6

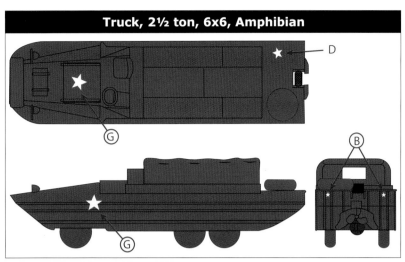

Truck, 2½ ton, 6x6, Amphibian

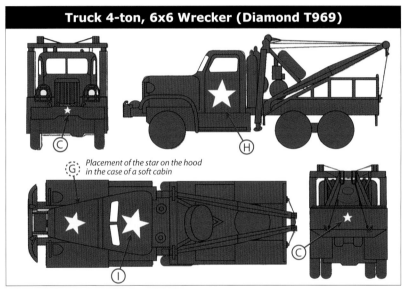

Truck 4-ton, 6x6 Wrecker (Diamond T969)

Placement of the star on the hood in the case of a soft cabin

Above.
June 16, 1944. Unloading in the artificial port at Omaha. This DUKW has two stars on its side, both done with a stencil. The color stripes of the unit's number code are next to the star at the back. (see chapter 5). (National Archives)

Below.
Near Crest (Drôme), August 1944. This Wrecker Diamond T belonged to the 734th Ordnance Battalion. Due to a lack of space, the O of Ordnance has been placed on the right-hand side of the bumper. Also visible are the circled stars on the bumper and the door. On the grille, the bridge classification plate shows two figures, whether the truck is towing another. (National Archives)

Truck, Cargo 4-ton, 6x6 (Diamond T968)

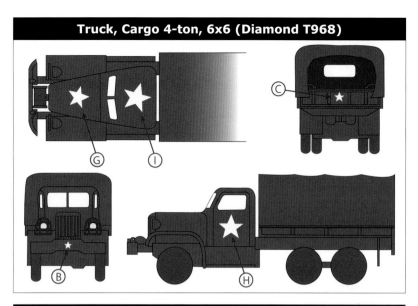

Truck Cargo 6-ton, 6x6 (Corbitt/White)

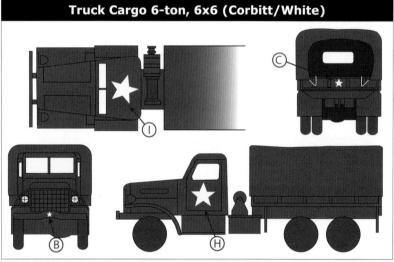

Tractor 4/5-ton, 4x4

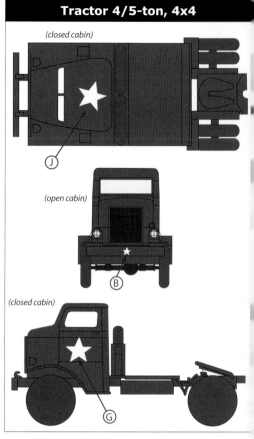

(closed cabin)

(open cabin)

(closed cabin)

Below.
These Autocar tractors, stocked in Great Britain before the landings, have had their markings repainted larger and in white on the engine compartment, with stencil and a paint gun. The small stars on the bumpers have been painted in the same way, as well as a yellow disk left empty. The use of antifreeze is indicated by the PRES 44 above the radiator.

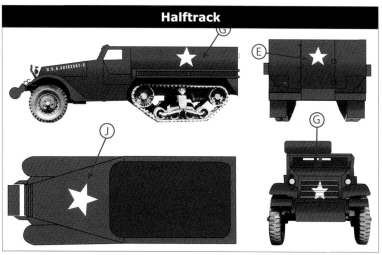

Halftrack

Above.
On a halftrack, an example of the yellow paint that detects vesicant gas, on the hood's available space and visible by the driver.

Right.
The stars on this M20 armored car of the 14th Armored Division are missing at the back, covered by dust on the side and hidden by impedimenta on the turret.

Below.
An M3 halftrack of the 2nd Armored Division in Normandy. Note that the stars on the body have been covered up.

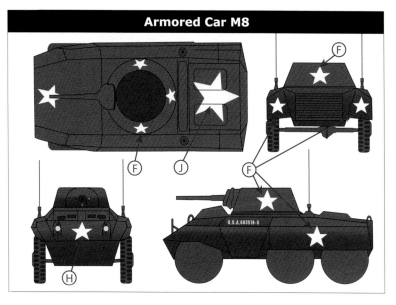

Armored Car M8

Light Tank M5

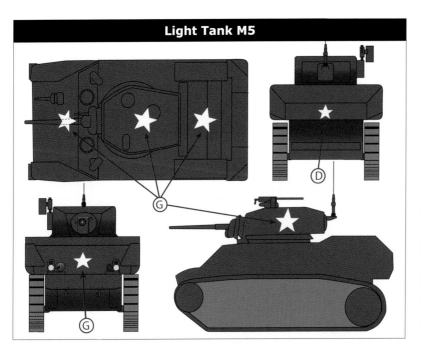

Medium Tank M4

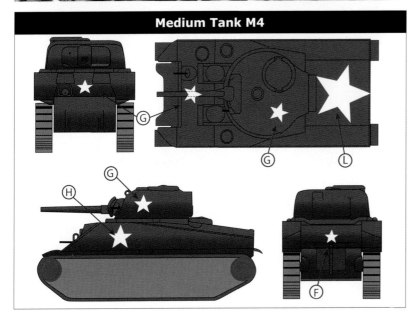

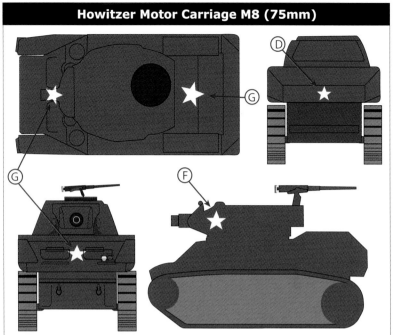

Howitzer Motor Carriage M8 (75mm)

Above, left.
A self-propelled M8 from the 106th Cavalry Reconnaissance Group in operation in Germany in February 1945. An additional circled star has been painted on the side of the machine.

Left.
A 105mm self-propelled M7 belonging to the 2nd Armored Division in England. The placement of the identification stars is as per regulations. Erased by the censor, the unit markings on the left identify the 14th, 78th or the 92nd Armored Field Artillery Battalion.

Howitzer Motor Carriage M7 (105mm)

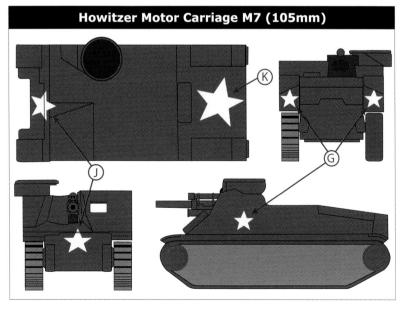

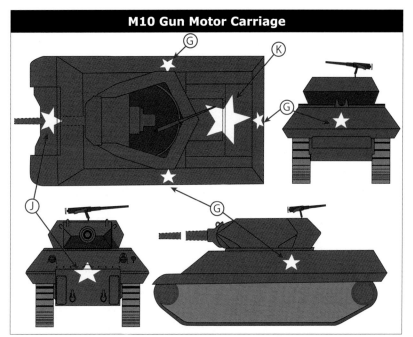

M10 Gun Motor Carriage

Above.
This M4 artillery tractor towing a 155mm gun in Germany, belongs to the 261st Field Artillery Battalion of
the Ninth Army. It is the 1st machine of Battery B.

1A 634TD

Left.
An M10 tank destroyer of the 634th Tank Destroyer Battalion, during the fight for Aix-la-Chapelle (Aachen) in October 1944. The star on the front slope is almost covered by the sandbags and the marks on the sides and the turret are invisible. On the left fender is the yellow disk indicating the tank's bridge classification number: 30, or 32 with an armored ammunition trailer.

Below.
A Pacific M26 tractor during an exercise in Great Britain before the landings. The unit markings on the front have been masked by the censor.
(National Archives)

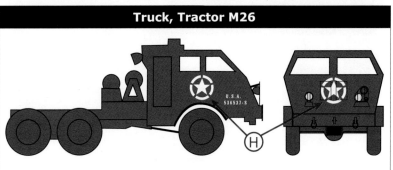

Truck, Tractor M26

High-Speed Tractors

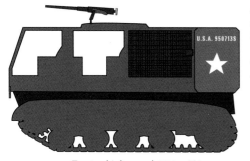

U.S.A. 934446-S

Tractor, high-speed, 36-ton M6

U.S.A. 950713S

Tractor, high-speed, 18-ton M4

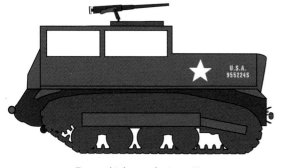

U.S.A.
955224S

Tractor, high-speed, 13-ton M5

Note. These tractors did not exist when the first edition of the AR 850-5 was published. The February 1945 additions only indicate that the white star markings should conform to those machines of the same type and size.

Trailers

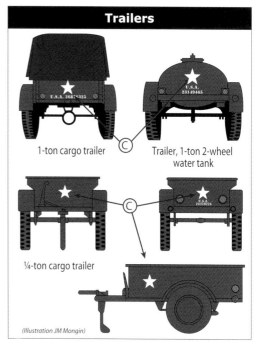

U.S.A. 26870325

1-ton cargo trailer

U.S.A. 23149465

Trailer, 1-ton 2-wheel water tank

U.S.A. 29378326

¼-ton cargo trailer

(Illustration JM Mongin)

Above.
Detail of the star and registration number on the side of an M4 tractor, during the winter of 1944.

Left.
During Operation Cobra, *an 8in M1 howitzer is being pulled by an M4 tracked tractor. Note the stars on the sides and rear of the body.*
(National Archives)

Usage Markings

A Jeep of the 320th Glider Field Artillery Battalion (82nd Airborne Division) is being loaded onto a Waco glider in 1943. On the left of the grille is the yellow disk that indicates the category of the engineer bridge that can support this vehicle.

In addition to the markings already presented, there were also other markings—we will refer to them as usage markings.

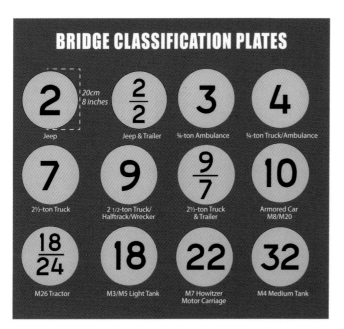

BRIDGE CLASSIFICATION PLATES

2 (20cm 8 inches)	**2/2**	**3**	**4**
Jeep	Jeep & Trailer	¾-ton Ambulance	¾-ton Truck/Ambulance
7	**9**	**9/7**	**10**
2½-ton Truck	2 1/2-ton Truck/ Halftrack/Wrecker	2½-ton Truck & Trailer	Armored Car M8/M20
18/24	**18**	**22**	**32**
M26 Tractor	M3/M5 Light Tank	M7 Howitzer Motor Carriage	M4 Medium Tank

These were bridge classification markings required to cross pontoon bridges built by the engineers: tonnage and displacement markings for maritime loads, and technical signage. But these were far from being systematic: replacement vehicles allocated during the campaign or repaired by workshops of the Ordnance Department, as well as those coming directly from the United States without going through Great Britain, often bore few markings; although the numbers of the landing ships and craft bound for Normandy—inscribed with chalk on the bumpers or any vertical part of a vehicle—were often highly visible.

Bridge Classification Plates

This was the system in place in the British Army from 1938, and adopted in 1943 by the U.S. Army. It categorized bridges depending on total weight, but also the load distribution on the axles, and the speed and the spacing of the vehicles and machines that they could support. Vehicles were subjected to the same classification and only those vehicles with classifications less than or equal to a bridge's could cross.

The number stating the classification (which was therefore different to the weight of the machine) was painted black on a bright yellow disk, to the right at the front, or directly on the body. A number atop another indicated a trailer.

After February 1945, these marking were no longer compulsory for vehicles with a payload less than 1½ tons (excepting local directives).

Top.
March 30, 1945, Germany. A Pershing T-26 heavy tank crosses a Treadway bridge positioned over the Rhine at Wesel. Note the yellow disk on the poles, indicating the bridge classification (40).
(National Archives)

Middle.
October 1944 in eastern France, an engineer unit pumps water from a river. The 1-ton trailer on the left shows a 6/2 classification marking.

Bottom, left.
A 4-ton Diamond T artillery tractor, with a 17/12 bridge classification on its bumper; the second number refers to the towed equipment.

Bottom, right.
June 1944, south of England, a column of vehicles waiting to be loaded on the vessels bound for Normandy. The GMC in the background has a classification plate of 7 and another plate mentioning the ship on which it must be loaded, a Landing Craft Tank (LCT).
(National Archives via J. Gawne)

Weight and Size Markings for Shipping

All vehicles and machines boarding for overseas should—in principle—display the proper markings: dimensions (length, width, height), road weight and gross weight.

These markings, which varied in their execution, were made with white paint on the vertical side of the vehicle (usually the left for Jeeps), and one or two inches high, depending on the dimensions of the vehicle.

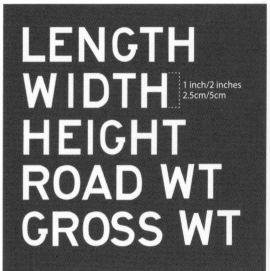

LENGTH
WIDTH
HEIGHT
ROAD WT
GROSS WT

1 inch/2 inches
2.5cm/5cm

Top.
Shipping markings on an M5A1 light tank of the 102nd Cavalry Reconnaissance Squadron. The driver, Sergeant Curtis Culin, is the inventor of the hedge-cutting device that was used in front of the tanks in Normandy. The EQ weight corresponds to the weight in fighting order.

Left.
Servicing trucks of the Red Ball Express in a workshop. The dimensions and tonnage markings painted on the cabin of this 2½-ton truck are as follows:
O LGTH 21 FT 4 IN (Overall length)
O WIDTH 7 FT 4 IN (Overall width)
BED HGT 6FT 3 IN (Bed Height)
3 TON CWT (payload, expressed in volumetric weight)

Above, left.
This Jeep trailer, belonging to the air force, displays the dimensions and weight markings at the front.

Above, right.
Spring 1944, during landings rehearsals, these vehicles from the 102nd Cavalry Reconnaissance Squadron are waiting to disembark. Note the driving and maximum authorized speed markings for Britain, on the tailgates of the two GMCs.

Left.
On a landing craft, shortly before departure for Normandy. Recommendations for driving in Britain are painted on the tarpaulin at the back of the Jeep. Such dispositions did not apply to the vehicles coming directly to the continent from the U.S. On the Jeep in the foreground, the gaps between the star and the circle are filled with yellow vesicant-detection paint.

Maximum Authorized Speed

This safety measure was indicated in miles per hour (MPH) at the back of the vehicle, in two- or three-inch-high characters. It was sometimes repeated on the dashboard (see page 142).
Examples:
– M8 Armored Car: Max Speed 20 mph (32 kph)
– Jeep: Max Speed 40 mph (64 kph)
– ¾-ton truck: Max Speed 30 mph (48 kph)
– 2½-ton truck: Max Speed 30 mph (48 kph)

Driving Mode Indicators

HQ ETOUSA's (European Theater of Operations United States Army) 15th circular, February 16, 1943, stipulated that American vehicles driving in Great Britain (on the left-hand side) and without indicators, must display the following markings at the back, in white letters at least 1½ inches high, as per the model below:

Automobile Plates

Metallic and affixed to the right of the bumper and to the left at the back, these automobile plates were of two kinds: the ones identifying the headquarters of a major unit (brigade and above), and those identifying the vehicle of a general. The dimensions were 22.5 x 15 cm.

Antifreeze

Protection of the radiator against the cold by adding antifreeze was indicated. The brand of the product used was indicated (Prestone, Pres) or the words Anti-Freeze followed by the year of validity. This marking was painted at the front of the hood in one- to three-inch-high white lettering.

Personalization

Pin-ups were permitted with command agreement. In no way were they to upset any puritanical values in the U.S. Personal markings were mostly benign inscriptions and illustrations, the first name of a girlfriend, the name of the state the crew came from, or characters taken from a Walt Disney movie.

Waterproofing Checklist

In planning for the Normandy landings and in order to allow the vehicles to drive in shallow waters during the disembarkation, engines were waterproofed with a thick asbestos-based paste, a coating that had to be

Above.
England, May 1944. This M20 armored car of the 821st Tank Destroyer Battalion, displays the speed limit and left-hand-driving markings.

Below.
During maneuvers of the Third Army in the States, in July 1943, Major General W.D. Crittenberger, Commanding Officer of the III Armored Corps, poses in front of his vehicle.
Note the rank plate (two stars), affixed to the side of the fender, and the blue and white unit plate on the front, with CG for Commanding General.

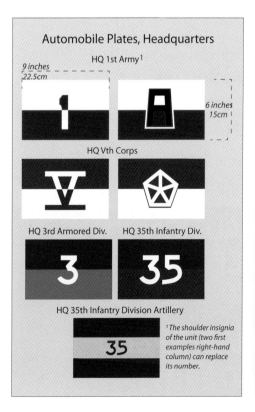

Automobile Plates, Headquarters

HQ 1st Army[1]

9 inches
22.5cm

6 inches
15cm

HQ Vth Corps

HQ 3rd Armored Div.   HQ 35th Infantry Div.

3   35

HQ 35th Infantry Division Artillery

35

[1] The shoulder insignia of the unit (two first examples right-hand column) can replace its number.

Automobile Plates, General officers

Brigadier General   Major General   Lieutenant General   General

removed on dry land. Only the machines which could display proof of waterproofing on their windshields—a rectangular sticker of the American flag, with initials of the officer in charge of checking the preparations on the front, and on the back the instructions relating to the reverse process—were allowed to be loaded.

Below.
June 17, 1945, Czechoslovakia. General Patton reviews the 301st Infantry, 94th Division. For the occasion, the personal Jeep of General Fortier, commanding officer of the division, displays the plate with the four stars of its illustrious passenger.

Above, left
A GMC of the Red Ball Express decorated with German machine-gun belts and a pin-up on the windshield.

Inset.
A pin-up from a contemporary American illustrated magazine.

Above.
Preparing for Normandy. Note the sticker indicating the waterproofing checklist on the windshield of a Jeep from the Military Police Platoon of the 1st Division.
(National Archives via Jon Gawne)

Below.
Belgium, January 1945, this ambulance of the 312th Medical Battalion from the 87th Division has received the Prestone 45 markings on the front of its hood, indicating the use of antifreeze.

Examples of antifreeze indication

Ambulances

1943, at an airbase in England. This ambulance of the 386th Bombardment Group / 554 Bombardment Squadron (Medium) carries the regulation unit markings on the bumper. Note also the X prefix, added before the registration number on the hood, which means that the vehicle was completely rebuilt or that its original registration number was unknown. In the case of this ½-ton WC27 ambulance, it is almost certain that it was equipment given to the British as part of the Lend-Lease agreement and then returned in Britain. The 7 indicates the class of the vehicle, the 1047th model of this category, registered in this way.
(National Archives)

The unit markings painted on the front bumper and on the two "bumperettes" at the back of the ¾-ton ambulances follow the regulations explained in chapter 5, the second group displaying the M for Medical after the unit number. The abbreviations of the third group are shown in the text box on page 74.

Neutrality Markings

Most instructions and marking regulations dealt with in this book originated from fall 1943 (U.S.A. regulations) and from early 1944 (U.S. high command in Great Britain). They are illustrated on the next page. Note that the cross on the back doors covered the registration number.

Ambulances from the veterinary service carried the same markings—though with green crosses— except for the roof and the back of the main body, and no emblem.

An addition from February 1945 indicated that vehicles other than ambulances but that were used as such, and whose appearance did not exclude protection from the Geneva Convention, had to be signaged in the same way as ambulances. This was the case for Jeeps and some halftracks, amongst others, used at the front to evacuate the wounded.

Circular HQ ETO of January 24, 1944 only allowed one white star on the roof, and the marking *Ambulance* above the windshield was removed. On June 15, 1944, a decision from the same source suppressed the star on the roof of ambulances, surgery trucks, and blood bank trucks. The photographs of the time show that these dispositions were not always observed. The marking Left Hand Drive showed on some ambulances, half on the right of the red cross's white background, and half on the curve of the body.

THE MEDICAL DETACHMENT

Each infantry division had a medical battalion, which assigned personnel to each regiment. The medical detachment attached to each infantry regiment was generally divided in three sections. At its disposal were seven Jeeps with trailers and a 2½-ton truck.

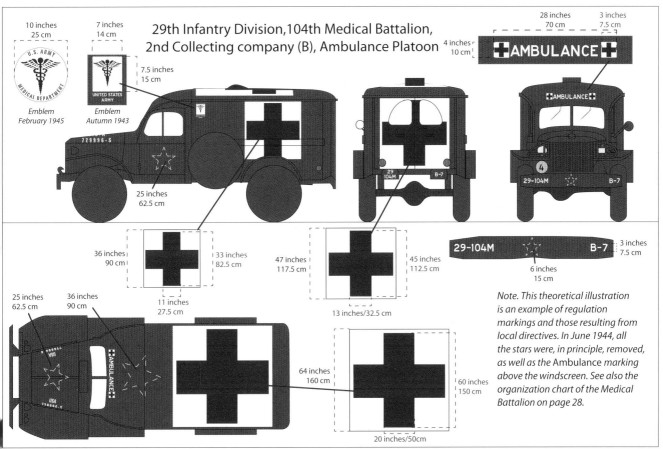

29th Infantry Division, 104th Medical Battalion, 2nd Collecting company (B), Ambulance Platoon

10 inches / 25 cm — Emblem February 1945

7 inches / 14 cm — Emblem Autumn 1943

7.5 inches / 15 cm

729996-S

25 inches / 62.5 cm

4 inches / 10 cm

28 inches / 70 cm — 3 inches / 7.5 cm

✚AMBULANCE✚

✚AMBULANCE✚

29 104M — B-7

4

29-104M — B-7

36 inches / 90 cm — 33 inches / 82.5 cm

11 inches / 27.5 cm

47 inches / 117.5 cm — 45 inches / 112.5 cm

13 inches/32.5 cm

29-104M ★ B-7 — 3 inches / 7.5 cm

6 inches / 15 cm

25 inches / 62.5 cm — 36 inches / 90 cm

64 inches / 160 cm — 60 inches / 150 cm

20 inches/50cm

Note. This theoretical illustration is an example of regulation markings and those resulting from local directives. In June 1944, all the stars were, in principle, removed, as well as the Ambulance marking above the windscreen. See also the organization chart of the Medical Battalion on page 28.

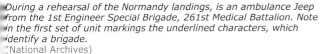

During a rehearsal of the Normandy landings, is an ambulance Jeep from the 1st Engineer Special Brigade, 261st Medical Battalion. Note in the first set of unit markings the underlined characters, which identify a brigade.
(National Archives)

This Jeep carries the markings of the Medical Detachment (MD) of the 119th Infantry Regiment, 30th Infantry Division. Note the red cross on a white background painted on the grille.
(National Archives via. J. Gawne)

Above.
In the Rhône Valley, summer 1944, a medic of the 36th Division gives a drink to a wounded German. Note the Jeep trailer in the background, marked with two red crosses on a white disk.
(National Archives)

Above.
The Ardennes, December 1944. Medics from the 60th Infantry Regiment, 9th Infantry Division load a wounded soldier into a halftrack ambulance of the 32nd Armored Regiment's Medical Detachment, 3rd Armored Division.
(National Archives)

Right.
An ambulance from the 29th Division's Medical Battalion in the Saint-Lô sector, July 1944. Note the larger red crosses above the cab, the absence of white stars, and the flag at the front of the vehicle.

Left.
The Ardennes, December 1944. This Jeep also belongs to the Medical Detachment of the 32nd Armored Regiment, 3rd Armored Division, whose markings are displayed on the bumper. Large crosses are painted on the modified fenders, the grille, on the windshield's frame, and the sides.
(National Archives)

3RD GROUP UNIT MARKINGS, MEDICAL DEPARTMENT (SEE ALSO PAGE 81)

COLL	Collecting (Company)
CLR	Clearing (Company)
CONV	Convalescent (Hospital)
EV, EVAC	Evacuation (Hospital)
GEN	General (Hospital)
FLD	Field (Hospital)
LAB	Laboratory
SAN	Sanitary (Company)
STA	Station (Hospital)
SUR	Surgical (Hospital)
VET	Veterinary

Above.
Placement of markings on ambulances of the 65th Medical Battalion, XV Corps, waiting to load patients who are to be air-evacuated.
(National Archives)

Right.
Summer 1944 in Italy, an ambulance of the 1st Tank Battalion's medical detachment, 1st Armored Division.

Below.
France 1945, an ambulance assigned to transport wounded to airfields for air evacuation. The markings of the 477th Medical Ambulance Company are inverted. They should read ASCZ (Advance Section Com Z), 477M, AMB 13.
(National Archives)

EXAMPLES OF MEDICAL DEPARTMENT VEHICLE MARKINGS

ASCZ-28M **GEN 12**

Advance Section Com Z, 28th General Hospital, 12th vehicle

82AB-307M **3**

82nd Airborne Division, 307th Medical Company, 3rd vehicle

3A-587M **AMB6**

Third Army, 587th Motor Ambulance Company, 6th vehicle

2△-82R **MED 28**

2nd Armored Division, 82nd Armored Reconnaissance Battalion, Medical Detachment, 28th vehicle

91-316M **D-6**

91st Infantry Division, 316th Medical Battalion, Clearing Company, 6th vehicle

1A-1M **DP-7**

First Army, 1st Medical Depot, 7th vehicle

3△-32△ **M-3**

3rd Armored Div., 32nd Armored Regiment, Medical Detachment (halftrack)

PBS-833M ★ **COLL 13**

Peninsular Base Section, 833rd Medical Battalion, Collecting Co., 13th vehicle

Sicily, July 1943, this halftrack ambulance christened "Mid-forceps" probably belonged to a medical detachment of the 2nd Armored Division. The neutrality markings show on the side of the body, at the back, and on the flag at the front.
(National Archives)

The Military Police

Whether for maintaining public order, security, traffic regulation or convoy escort missions, the military police had to be highly visible, and their vehicles clearly identifiable with the wording Military Police in addition to the regulation bumper markings.

Left.
From 1942, Cheltenham (Gloucestershire) was the HQ of the Service of Supply (SOS) American forces in Great Britain (future ETOUSA). Here is part of the MP section in December 1943.
(National Archives via J. Gawne)

EXAMPLES OF MILITARY POLICE MARKINGS

3A-503P ★ B-16
Third Army, 503rd MP Battalion, B Company, 16th vehicle

ASCZ 783 P HQ 11
Advance Section Com Z, 783rd MP Battalion, HQ Co., 11th vehicle

1A-518P ★ C-7
First Army, 518th MP Battalion, C Company, 7th vehicle

3A-503P ★ B-16
Third Army, 503rd MP Battalion, B Company, 16th vehicle

1ESₚ 449P ★ 5
1st Engineer Special Brigade, 449th Military Police Co., 5th vehicle

5ESB 210 P ★ 9
5th Engineer Special Brigade, 210th Military Police Company

Late 1945 in Reims, in the Oise Section of the Com Z, a radio Jeep and an Indian motorcycle from the 726th MP Battalion.
(National Archives via J. Gawne)

Left.
A multinational patrol in Vienna in 1945. This Jeep from the 505th MP Battalion has been repainted with several types of stencils for the unit markings on the bumper.

Right.
March 1945 in Germany, an unidentified 2½-ton truck of the 11th Armored Division is assigned to POW transport, hence the "Military Police" on the grille. MP platoons did not own vehicles of such tonnage.

The Clubmobile

The Clubmobile truck was a kind of soldiers' social center on wheels, managed by American Red Cross staff to bring coffee, donuts and a feminine smile to the troops on campaign. In England, AEC-modified London buses were used, but for operations after D-Day on the continent, modified GMC 2½-ton Army trucks were also employed.

WC 62 6x6 Cinemobiles from the ARC were also used to show movies.

Above, right.
One of the first Clubmobiles lands in Normandy in June 1944; it is painted in the same gray as the British buses.

Below.
The Bookmobile was a traveling library, managed by the army through the Army Hostess and Librarian Service of the Special Services.

Right.
A Clubmobile pays a visit to the G.I.s of the 44th Division in the east of France in March 1945. It is painted Olive Drab and displays its military registration.

Bottom left.
A Clubmobile in Normandy, July 1944.

Below.
Near the end of the war, in Germany, a Clubmobile crew serving troops from the 87th Infantry Division, whose insignia is painted on the body, along with the name of the driver and the two "Donut Dollies."

UNIT MARKINGS

29-115-I-AT-6   29-115-I-HQ-7

Army Regulations AR-850-5 of August 5, 1942, also defined the markings that allowed the identification of the organization to which the vehicle belonged.

Regulation Unit Markings

These markings were painted on the front and back of vehicles and machines. The paint used was white, with petrol employed as a solvent for the pigments, so as to be able to quickly erase the markings with the same product.

Regulation unit markings consisted of four groups of digits and characters, read horizontally from left to right, on one or two lines depending on the space available and the configuration of the vehicle. The characters, whose dimensions were standardized, were three inches high, sometimes separated by an inch-long hyphen. The list of authorized unit abbreviations is displayed on page 82.

- The characters of the **first group** indicated the appropriate organization such as: division, corps, army, army group, air force, Com Z, Army Ground Forces, Army Service Forces, brigade, etc. Note in particular that brigades (engineer, artillery, etc.) were identified by a white horizontal stripe beneath these markings.
- The **second group** indicated a regiment, a brigade, a group, a battalion or a company/battery/platoon, whose number was followed by a symbol, or letters, identifying the arm or service. In the case of the HQ, or smaller units directly subordinated to the HQ (in a division: signals, ordnance, quartermaster, chaplains, etc.), the second group only included an X. The exact nature of this smaller unit was specified by the third group.

V-190F   I-HQ

SHAPES AND DIMENSIONS OF LETTERS AND NUMBERS

ABCDEF
GHIJKLM
NOPQRST
UVWXYZ
12345
67890 -

3 inches
7 cm

1 inch
2.5 cm

October 1944, near Nancy, a motorcycle from the 6th Cavalry Group of the Third Army.
(National Archives via J. Gawne)

- The **third group** identified the company or the unit of equivalent size (such as battery in the artillery, or troop in the mechanized cavalry).
- The **fourth group** included the number of the vehicle or machine within its unit. If applicable, its trailer would be numbered in succession. For example: Jeep: vehicle no. 9, trailer: no. 10.

Remember that to identify a unit based on a vehicle's markings, it is essential to have the precise information on the U.S. order of battle, as different units from a similar arm or service could have the same number. For example, in the artillery, a field artillery group, field artillery regiment, or field artillery battalion would all be identified by an F in the second group. Conversely, once you have chosen the unit for your restored vehicle, you should ensure that it did have on its inventory this type of vehicle or machine at the time; refer to the organization tables in chapter 3.

Italy, General Devers next to his Jeep, with the markings of II Army Corps HQ on the bumper, as well as two metal plates, one on a red background for the rank and the other white and blue, identifying the command post of II Corps (see page 70). Note also the uneven shape of the letters and figures.

UNIT MARKINGS EXPLANATION

Note: in the examples below, for more clarity, the white stars have been omitted from the notional bumpers.

Concept: the markings are divided in four groups

1st group: Identification of the larger unit or organization

2nd group: regiment, battalion, squadron etc.

3rd group: company or unit of similar level (battery, troop)

4th group: vehicle no. in battle order

national marking

`82A/B-307E ★ HQ2` — 2 inches / 7.5 cm

82nd Airborne Division | 307th Airborne Engineer Battalion | HQ : Headquarters Company | Vehicle no. 2

Specific example of the HQ and units directly attached to the HQ of the larger unit (such as army, corps, division etc.)

`4-X ★ HQ-3`

4th Infantry Division | HQ : Headquarters Company | Vehicle no. 3

`102-X ★ 102Q-8`

102nd Infantry Division | Quartermaster Company | Vehicle no. 8

Examples of markings from the <u>first group</u>

12GP
ARMY GROUPS: Twelfth Army Group (Arabic numerals)

3A
ARMY: Third Army (Arabic numerals)

XIX
ARMY CORPS: XIX Army Corps (Roman numerals)

8★
AIR FORCE: Eighth Air Force (here, the star indicates the Army Air Forces)

29
INFANTRY DIVISION: 29th Infantry Division
The "I" of Infantry does not appear in the first group markings

3△
ARMORED DIVISION: 3rd Armored Division

17A/B
AIRBORNE DIVISION: 17th Airborne Division

1ESp
BRIGADE: 1st Engineer Special Brigade

COMZ
COMMUNICATION ZONE

Examples of markings from the <u>second group</u>

12GP 2RNGR
Twelfth Army Group, 2nd Ranger Battalion

3A-489AAA
Third Army, 489th Antiaircraft Artillery Battalion

V-602TD
V Corps, 602nd Tank Destroyer Battalion

9★474FG
Ninth Air Force, 474th Fighter Group

29-116-I
29th Infantry Division, 116th Infantry Regiment

2△-67△
2nd Armored Division, 67th Armored Regiment

101A/B-502-I
101st Airborne Division, 502nd Parachute Infantry Regiment

1ESp-261M
1st Engineer Special Brigade, 261st Medical Battalion

ASCZ 4006 TC
Advance Section Communication Zone, 4006th Truck Company, Quartermaster Corps

Note. These examples reflect the theory of the regulation for some, but also the reality for others, as it was not always respected. There existed some variations as to the shape of the numbers and letters, depending on the stencils available, but also in the composition of the markings: missing elements, like the white hyphen that separated the groups, or that helped avoid confusion between the number 1 and the letter I, or the number 0 and the letter O.

Examples of markings from the third and fourth groups

1A 2RNGR   HQ-15
First Army, 2nd Ranger Battalion, HQ Company, 15th vehicle

3A-761△   A2
Third Army, 761st Tank Battalion (Separate),, A Company, 2nd machine

1A-87G   C6
First Army, 87th Chemical Mortar Battalion, C Company, 6th machine

VIII-13FOB   A-26
VIII Corps, 13th Field Artillery Observation Battalion, A Battery, 26th machine

9★474FG   430FS-1
Ninth Air Force, 474th Fighter Group, 430th Fighter Squadron, 1st vehicle

5-11-1   3HQ-10
5th Infantry Division, 11th Infantry Regiment, 3rd Battalion HQ, Company, 10th machine

9-15E-B-35
9th Infantry Division, 15th Engineer Combat Battalion, B Company, 35th machine

90X   P-10
90th Infantry Division, Special Troops, Military Police Platoon, 10th vehicle

5△-85C   B3
5th Armored Division, 85th Cavalry Reconnaissance Squadron, Troop B, 3rd machine

7△ 38-1   B12
7th Armored Division, 38th Armored Infantry Battalion, B Company, 12th machine

82A/B-320F   A-8
82nd Airborne Division, 320th Glider Field Artillery Battalion, A Battery, 8th vehicle

COMZ-523Q   B-4
Communications Zone, 523rd Quartermaster Battalion, B Company, 4th vehicle

At the Desert Training Center this halftrack displays the markings of a small unit that was subordinate to the IV Armored Corps' HQ.
(National Archives via. J. Gawne)

At the beginning of the war, a ½-ton Dodge weapons carrier displays the double markings painted on its tailgate and bumperettes, for the 70th Engineer Battalion, First Army.

Algeria, November 1943. This rare 1½-ton, 40-x2 COE kitchen truck was assigned to the 58th Mobile Medical Battalion of the Mediterranean Base Section (MBS), as the 17th HQ vehicle. The bumper is partially painted white to be more visible by night, and a plate showing the name of the driver is mounted on the front right fender.

Unit Markings
Authorized abbreviations and symbols

1st group

A	Army
AA	Antiaircraft
AAF	Army Air Forces
★	Air Force[1]
AAF TCC	AAF Troop Carrier Command
AB, A/B, ABN	Airborne
AGp/GP	Army Group
AGF	Army Ground Forces
ASF	Army Service Forces
COMZ (CZ)	Communications Zone
ESB	Engineer Special Brigade
ETO	European Theater of Operations
GHQ	General Headquarters (USA, before 1942)
NBS	Normandy Base Section
PBS	Peninsular Base Section (Italy)
SHAEF	Supreme Headquarters, Allied Expeditionary Forces
SOS	Services of Supply
SSF	Special Service Force
USF /USFET	US Forces European Theater, replaced SHAEF in 1945
Δ	Armored

2nd group

AA(A)	Antiaircraft Artillery
AB (A/B)	Airborne
ADSEC	Advance Section Com Z
AFSC	Air Force Service Command
AM	Amphibious
ASCZ	Advance Section Com Z
Δ	Armored
BBS	Brittany Base Section
BD	Berlin District
BW	Bombardment Wing
BG	Bombardment Group
BS	Bombardment Squadron
C	Cavalry
CA	Coast Artillery (DCA)
CB	Continental Base Section
CBS	Central Base Section (GB)

CCU	Combat Camera Unit (Air Force)
E	Engineer
ENGR	Engineer
FG	Fighter Group
F	Field Artillery
FW	Fighter Wing
FG	Fighter Group
FS	Fighter Squadron
G	Chemical (Gas)
GLI	Glider Infantry
GPSV	Service Group (AAF)
-I	Infantry
LS	Loire Base Section Com Z
M	Medical
MN	Mountain
MTS	Motor Transport Service
NBS	Normandy Base Section
OS	Oise Section
P	Military Police
Q	Quartermaster
-O	Ordnance
OB	(Field) Observation Battalion (Artillery)
R	Reconnaissance
S	Signal
SBS	Southern Base Section (GB)
T	Truck
TC	Transportation Corps/Truck Co.
TD	Tank Destroyer
TN	Divisional trains, Armored Div.
X	Headquarters (division or larger unit, or a smaller unit from the third group that is attached directly to the HQ)

3rd group

AM	Ammunition
AMB	Ambulance
AT	Antitank
AV	Aviation[2]
CAR	Car (QMC)
CLR	Clearing (Co. Medical Bn)
CN	Cannon
COLL	Collecting (Co. Medical Bn)
CON	Construction
DP	Depot
EV	Evacuation (Hospital)

FF	Fire Fighting
FLD	Field Hospital
DS	Direct Support
G	Chemical
GEN	General (Hospital)
GS	General Support
GR	Graves Registration
HQ	Headquarters, HQ Co./HQ and Service Co.
HW	Heavy Weapons
LAB	Laboratory
P	Military Police
MR	Mortar
MD	Medical Detachment
MED (M)	Medical
MTC	Motor Transport
MT	Maintenance
LDY	Laundry
OPN	Operations (Signal Corps)
PHOTO	Photographic (Signal Corps)
PM	Parachute Maintenance
R	Reconnaissance
REF/REFG	Refrigeration (QMC)
REP	Repair
RHD	Railhead (QMC)
RNGR	Ranger
RP	Repair
RT	Rocket
SA	Sales (QMC)
SAN	Sanitary
SPC	Signal Photographic Company
SQ	Squadron (Air Force)
STA	Station (Hospital)
SUR	Surgical (Hospital)
SV	Service
TN	Train
T/TC	Transportation/Truck Company
TCC	Troop Carrier Command (Air Force)
TRK	Truck
VET	Veterinary (Hospital)
W	Weapons

Notes
[1] Confusing symbol, replaced in September 1945 by winged propellers within a circle.
[2] Refers to support units assigned to air forces (for example Aviation Engineers).

February 17, 1945, the 3rd Battalion of the 253rd Infantry, 63rd Infantry Division, makes a U-turn on a road blocked by mines. On the left, a 1½-ton 6x6 truck, towing a 57mm antitank gun is the 12th vehicle of the 3rd Battalion's HQ Company. The type of vehicle and the organization table on page 26 allow us to see that it belonged to the antitank platoon. The black marking is unknown. The cherry-colored air reconnaissance panel is attached to the hood (see page 142).
(National Archives via J. Gawne)

Above.
September 1944, General Barton, commander of the 4th Infantry Division, is driving a Jeep bearing the divisional HQ markings and the stars of his rank.

Left.
July 30, 1944, a self-propelled M7 drives through Coutances. The markings painted on the MG cupola are those of Battery B, 66th Armored Field Artillery Battalion, 4th Armored Division.

Below.
August 1944, in Saint-Malo, a Dodge truck equipped with speakers broadcasts an invitation to the remaining German soldiers to surrender. The unit markings are those of the 3rd Mobile Recording and Broadcasting Company, attached to the First Army Group.
(National Archives via J. Gawne)

Below.
A Jeep of HQ Company, 753rd Tank Battalion in Italy. This was a 5th Army unit, although it is not mentioned in the markings.

BBS 196 O. ★   HQ 3

101AB-327-1 ★ MED-1

Above, left.
November 1944, the markings of Chaplain Captain Clark Wood's Jeep indicate that he worked with the men of the 196th Ordnance Battalion of the Brittany Base Section (BBS), Com Z. Note that the "O" of Ordnance is not followed by its usual hyphen, but by a dot.

Above, right.
In Coutances, Normandy, after a mine detonation on July 26, 1944. The Jeep has the markings of the 202nd Engineer Combat Battalion of the Third Army. Note the Maintenance Patrol sign, likely in white on red background, signaling a vehicle charged with checking the condition of the roads.

Left.
September 1944. Preparing for Operation Market Garden, in the Netherlands this ambulance Jeep bears the markings of the Medical Detachment of the 327th Glider Infantry. Note the MED instead of the regulatory M.

Left.
A Sherman from B Company of the 756th Battalion crossing a town in the south of France. Note the solid white triangle identifying an armored unit, which could be found on other battalions coming from Italy (see the Jeep on page 83). The second tank is a Duplex Drive. The battalion supported the 3rd Infantry Division during the landings in Provence.

Below.
A ¾–ton WC53 radio truck, 8th vehicle of the 226th Signal Operations Company, from the Seventh Army.
(portraitofwar.com)

 7A-226S   OPN-8

Left.
Near Venafro in Italy, April 1944. A halftrack of the DCA mounted with an M15. This M15 half-track bears the markings of the 443rd Antiaircraft Artillery Battalion's Battery A.

Below.
Right at the end of the war in Bavaria, is a convoy of the 106th Cavalry Reconnaissance Squadron from the Seventh Army.

7-A 106C   B-37

Below.
Though no longer listed on the organization tables of the armored divisions of September 1943, here is an M3 Scout Car seen during 12th Armored Division training. It bears the markings of the 119th Engineer Battalion.
(12th Armored Division Association)

Below.
A Jeep of the 3rd Signal Company, 3rd Infantry Division enters Marseille in August 1944. The markings are identical to another vehicle of the company photographed several weeks earlier (see page 22). According to regulations, for a company under command of Divisional HQ, the markings should read 3-X-3S.

Above.
1943, Third Army maneuvers in Louisiana. This M3 tank carries the unit markings of the 741st Tank Battalion, Company B's 5th vehicle. The 741st was a non-divisional battalion. Company B landed in Normandy on June 6, 1944, in support of the 1st Infantry Division, equipped with amphibious M4 Duplex Drive tanks.

Below.
This high-speed M5 tractor's markings, barely visible, are of the 773rd Field Artillery Battalion, Third Army. It is towing an 4.5in artillery piece.

83-329-I 3-HQ-1

Left.
In the west of France, summer 1944, a Jeep from the HQ section of the HQ Company, 3rd Battalion of the 329th Infantry Regiment (83rd Infantry Division).

Below.
January 21, 1943 in Salé (Morocco), northeast of Rabat, President Roosevelt reviews troops of the 3rd Infantry Division.
The markings on the Jeep's bumper identify the 13th vehicle of the 3rd Battalion's HQ Company, from the 30th Infantry Regiment. The matt blue registration— in small characters and with the American flag painted for the landings in North Africa, in November 1942—is visible on the hood.
(National Archives)

Examples of Unit Markings by Vehicle Type

Motorcycle, solo

Unit markings were most often on the mudguards, sometimes on the windshields, which were often removed in the units at the front.

Right.
July 1944, Normandy. This Harley-Davidson WLA carries the markings of the 33rd Armored Regiment HQ, from the 3rd Armored Division, confirmed by the unit serial number 42895 and the corresponding color stripes on the fender (see explanation on page 126 onwards). Also note the shipping markings on the toolbox.

The 3rd Armored was a heavy division with regiments instead of battalions for tanks and infantry. It therefore had motorcycles in HQ companies of tank regiments, and the divisional reconnaissance battalion.

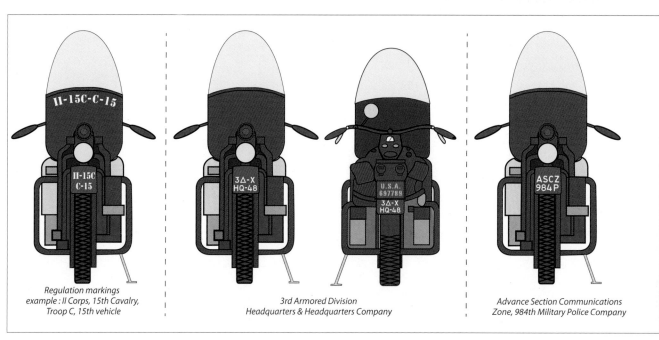

Regulation markings example : II Corps, 15th Cavalry, Troop C, 15th vehicle

3rd Armored Division Headquarters & Headquarters Company

Advance Section Communications Zone, 984th Military Police Company

Right.
Normandy, 1944. Solo motorcycle of the 2nd Armored Division, 82nd Reconnaissance Battalion, HQ's 87th vehicle. Note the unidentified colored stripes of the unit serial number above the unit markings.

Below, left.
202nd MP Company, II Corps, Fifth Army, Italy 1945 :

- Registration on the tank
- White star painted on a canvas covering the rear mudguard
- II Corps insignia on the front mudguard

Below, right.
General Clark's escort in Mostaganem in 1943. The motorcycles carry the markings of the Fifth Army's HQ, whose insignia is reproduced on windshields and helmets.
(National Archives via J. Gawne)

¼-ton Truck (Jeep)

Right.
Sicily, July 1943, a Jeep of the 7th Infantry (15th vehicle of the regiment's HQ company), from the 3rd Infantry Division enters Palermo. The unit markings are in keeping with regulations and are reproduced on the illustrations below. The three horizontal bars and letter are an unknown embarkation marking.
(National Archives)

3-7-1 ≡ A   HQ-15

★   3 7-1   HQ 15

Below, left.
Jeep from the 2nd Ranger Battalion (6th vehicle of the HQ company), in the Conquet Peninsula, August 1944. At that time, the battalion was a general reserve unit of the Twelfth Army Group. The Ranger battalion had very few organic vehicles; only nine Jeeps were allocated to the Supply & Transportation Section of the HQ Company.
(National Archives)

Below.
In the United States before departure for Europe, this Jeep belongs to a chaplain from the 75th Infantry Division, and carries the markings of Divisional HQ to which this officer was attached.
(National Archives)

12 AGP. 2 RNGR ★   HQ.6

Right.
Czechoslovakia, April 1945, seen here is a Jeep from Company H, 38th Infantry, 2nd Infantry Division. The markings in black on white on the bumper are reproduced below, the division's insignia replacing the star in the middle.

2-38-1 ★ H-17

Below.
Normandy, June 1944, a Jeep from the 261st Medical Battalion, 1st Engineer Special Brigade.

Below, right.
Italy, 1944. This Jeep carries on its back right bumperette, the unusual markings HS for the Headquarters and Service Company of the 109th Engineers, 34th Infantry Division.
(National Archives via J. Gawne)

Right.
A Jeep from Company A, 50th Armored Infantry Battalion, 6th Armored Division.

6△ 50-1 ★ A-11

Below.
A Jeep from the 353rd Infantry Regiment, 89th Infantry Division.

89·353·1 ★

Below.
A Jeep from the 85th Cavalry Reconnaissance Squadron, 5th Armored Division, Troop B's 19th vehicle

5△-85R B-19

Left.
For the parade of August 29, 1944 in Paris, the 28th Infantry Division represented the U.S. forces. This Jeep from the 110th Infantry Regiment carries the markings of the 2nd Battalion's HQ Company.

Below, left.
Bavaria, towards the end of the war. A Jeep from the 101st Airborne Division. The markings are those of the 327th Glider Infantry Regiment, 3rd Battalion HQ, according to the ace of clubs on the windshield. At that time, however, the 3rd Battalion of the 327th, was actually the 1/401st GIR.

Below, right.
This Jeep from the 466th Quartermaster Truck Company is accompanying truck convoys of the Red Ball Express established by the Advance Section Communications Zone.

28-110-1 ★ 2BN-4

Left.
End of January 1945, Belgium. Details of the markings at the back of a Jeep from the 307th Airborne Engineer Battalion's Company C, 82nd Airborne Division. Note the absence of the white star there.

Passenger Cars

Below.
Example of the Commanding General's sedan, 1st Armored Division.

¼-ton, 4x4 Amphibious Truck

Left.
Example of a vehicle from the HQ Company, 17th Armored Engineer Battalion, 2nd Armored Division.

Right.
The indifferent performance of the amphibious Jeep during the Sicilian landings dictated that it was palmed off to Lend-Lease beneficiaries. They were unusual in American units in Northwest Europe in 1944–45. This rare photograph, from Mark Bando's book on the 2nd Armored Division in Normandy, shows one of these cars, belonging to the reconnaissance company of the 67th Armored Regiment.

¾-ton Weapons Carrier Truck

A weapons carrier from the 126th Armored Ordnance Maintenance Battalion, 4th Armored Division in France, 1944. The star on the tailgate is hidden by the tool rack.

¾-ton Command & Reconnaissance Truck

Left.
Car, Command and Reconnaissance, 4x4, ¾-ton of HQ Company, V Corps in England. Note the marking LEFT HAND DRIVE that is displayed twice.

1½-ton Cargo Truck

Right.
Parade of August 29, 1944 on the Champs Elysées in Paris. The Truck Cargo 6x6 1½-ton is towing a 57mm antitank piece. The markings are those of the 112th Infantry Regiment's Antitank Company, 28th Infantry Division.

2½-ton, 6x6 Truck

Right.
July 1944, on the road from Périers to Coutances, a GMC from the Service Battery, 94th Armored Field Artillery Battalion, 4th Armored Division. The star on the bumper is of a smaller size because of the winch. The red sign on the radiator identifies the supplies being transported, to assist with convoy prioritization on the roads.

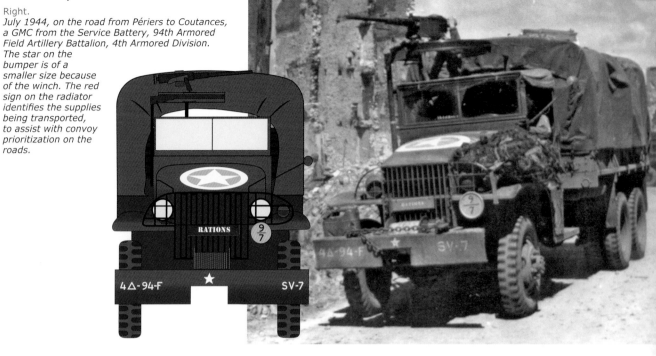

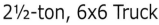

Below.
A tanker truck from the 405th Engineer Water Supply Battalion, a 5th Army unit in Italy.

Below.
Normandy, 1944. A truck of the Service Company, 357th Infantry, 90th Infantry Division is bringing troop reinforcements to the front. The unit markings are painted on the bumperettes; the left-hand drive notice painted in England still shows on the tailgate.
(National Archives)

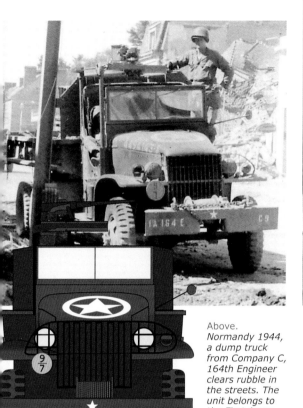

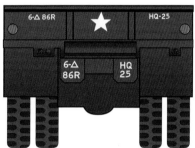

Above.
Normandy 1944,
a dump truck
from Company C,
164th Engineer
clears rubble in
the streets. The
unit belongs to
the First Army.

Above.
Brittany, 1944, a 2½-ton
truck of HQ Troop, 86th
Cavalry Reconnaissance
Squadron, 6th Armored
Division transporting
prisoners. The unit
markings show on
the tailgate and the
bumperettes.
(National Archives)

A 2½-ton cab-over-engine truck helps unload
a landing craft on a beach in Normandy.
The unit markings are those of the Advance
Section Com Z, 3882nd Truck Company,
operating for the Ordnance.
(National Archives)

Right.
Italy, 1944. This 1½-ton 4x4 Chevrolet truck belongs to the 1206th Engineer Composite Section, charged with, amongst other things, firefighting at the large depots exposed to air raids. The winch has been replaced by a water pump. Note the fire sign on the grille. Regulations state that Fire Department engines should be painted Fire Engine Red. Note also the blue registration number on the hood.

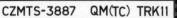

CZMTS-3887   QM(TC) TRK11

Left
This 4-ton open cabin tractor with trailer is being loaded with supplies at Cherbourg, at the end of the war. To make the vehicle more visible during nighttime convoys, the bumper is painted white with black markings.

Below.
This 2½-ton truck carrying a Le Roi compressor belongs to the 36th Engineer Combat Regiment in Italy. Its insignia (white and red emblem with a seahorse) is mounted on the grille, next to a diamond-shaped tactical sign, typical of this unit, and which also appears on the bumper.

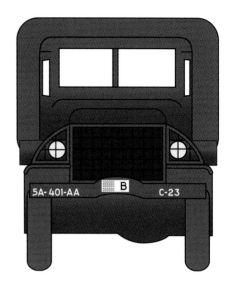

Left.
1944 at Gaeta Bay, near Naples. On the left is a 6-ton truck from the 401st Antiaircraft Artillery Gun Battalion (Mobile). These machines were used for towing heavy (90mm) AA pieces. Note in the middle of the bumper, the color stripes on the white background, displaying the unit number for tactical transport by sea.

Below.
In a depot at the rear in early 1945, this White or Corbitt truck is towing an LCVP landing craft in preparation of the Rhine crossing. The markings are Ninth Army, 625th Engineer, Light Equipment (LE) Company, vehicle no. 6. This type of highly mobile unit was equipped with tractors, cranes, and bulldozers to support engineer battalions in the staging areas.
(National Archives, via J. Gawne)

Below and right.
1945, this Diamond T wrecker belongs to a company of refrigerated trucks assigned to the blood bank. The markings on the bumper are those of the Com Z, Motor Transportation Service. Other photographs from the same series indicate that the unit is the 3601st QM Truck Co., whose markings are masked by the soldier. This company was equipped with 4- and 5-ton tractors with 10-ton refrigerated trailers (REFG). Note the Meritorious Unit citation (crown of laurels) on the right fender, and the emblem of the MTS on the left (see page 19).
(Portraitofwar.com)

453-AM-TRK-CO-23

2½-ton, 6x6 Amphibian Truck

Above.
Amphibious trucks of the 453rd Amphibian Truck Company, south of England, during a rehearsal for the Normandy landings.

Left and opposite, bottom.
66 "Ducks" from the 52nd Quartermaster Battalion (Mobile) on the Provence beaches in August 1944. The markings on the front left of the prow identify the LST which transported the vehicles from Nisida, an island near Napoli.

Right.
An amphibious truck from the 6th Engineer Special Brigade in Normandy. The markings under the windshield and on the hull are those of the 460th Amphibian Truck Company. Note the unit serial number 44415 in the center, above the three color stripes which complete this marking.

6ESB   44415   460AM

Right.
Markings on the back of another machine from the 460th Amphibian Truck Company, at Omaha Beach.

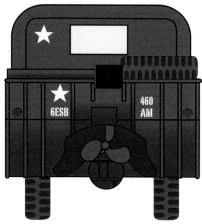

Tractors

An M26 tractor during the liberation of Le Mans, August 1944. The vehicle bears the markings of the Advance Section, Com Z, 78th Ordnance Base Group, 528th (Heavy Maintenance) Ordnance Company.
(Coll. Christophe Routier)

Another M26 tractor from the Normandy Base Section, Com Z, 37th vehicle of the 457th Ordnance Evacuation Company.

High-speed Tractor

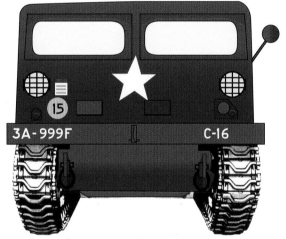

Above.
En route towards the loading ports to France, the 90mm AA guns of the 10th Antiaircraft Artillery (AAA) Gun Battalion, First Army, are being towed by M4 tracked vehicles. The serial number 45440 under the right headlight can easily be correlated with the unit markings on the bumper.
(National Archives via Jon Gawne)

Below.
A unit of black soldiers, the 999th Field Artillery Battalion, serving 240mm howitzers in the bridgehead of Mantes-Gassicourt. The pieces are towed by M4 tractors.

Below, right.
An M5 high-speed tractor towing an M1 155mm howitzer from the 9th Infantry Division, 34th Field Artillery Battalion, in the Cherbourg sector. Clearly visible are the stars on the tractor and the pin-up on the gun shield.
(National Archives)

Tractor, Track-type, Caterpillar D7

Right.
During the clearing-up of Cherbourg's port, seen here is a bulldozer belonging to the 1056th Engineer Port Construction and Repair Group. The serial unit number 32670 is stenciled on the grille, next to the corresponding color bars.
(National Archives)

Below.
August 1944, a Caterpillar D7 clears the road from Saint-Lô to Coutances. The markings of an engineer unit from the ASCZ, barely visible, are painted at the back of the flange of the pulley, the usual place for it.

Above.
Winter 1944 in the Ardennes. Seen here is a bulldozer with armored cabin belonging to the 305th Engineer Combat Battalion's Company A, 80th Division. The markings are painted on the cabin.
(National Archives)

Left.
September 1944, near Épinal, Company F from the 36th Engineer Combat Regiment is building a Bailey bridge. The markings are at the back, one of them a tactical marking typical of this regiment (see also page 98).
(National Archives)

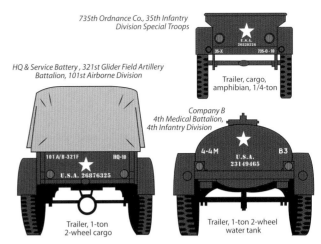

735th Ordnance Co., 35th Infantry
Division Special Troops

Trailer, cargo,
amphibian, 1/4-ton

HQ & Service Battery , 321st Glider Field Artillery
Battalion, 101st Airborne Division

Company B
4th Medical Battalion,
4th Infantry Division

Trailer, 1-ton
2-wheel cargo

Trailer, 1-ton 2-wheel
water tank

Trailers

Regulations stated that unit markings should be placed at the back of common trailers, but should be on the side for low and long models.

Above, left.
A hitch that was originally intended to evacuate tanks (truck trailer tank transporter 45-ton Diamond T prime mover M20) is being used on the Red Ball Express for supply transport. The trailer and tractor carry the markings ASCZ 3595 TC = Advance Section Com Z, 3595th Truck Company at the back. The registration number is painted on the side.
(National Archives)

Right.
Germany 1945, an M-10 ammunition trailer, belonging to the 920th Field Artillery Battalion (105mm), 95th Infantry Division, Service Battery (SV), 8th vehicle.

Carrier, Cargo, M29

Above, left.
Amphibious carrier M29C from the 97th Signal Battalion, a unit directly attached to XVI Corps.
(National Archives)

Left.
M29 carrier, from the 87th Chemical Mortar Battalion, First Army in Normandy. The 2½-ton truck belongs to the same unit, HQ's 18th machine.

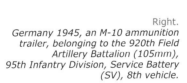

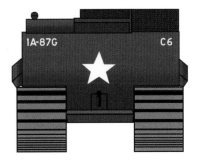

M8/20
Armored Car

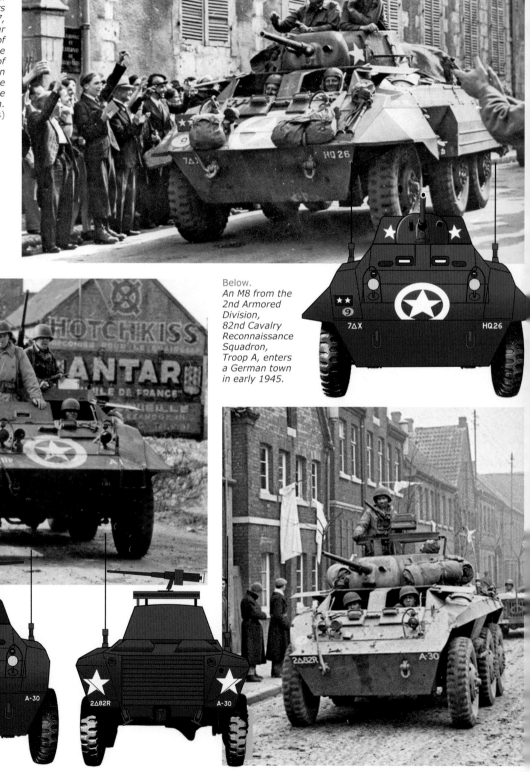

Right.
General Sylvester, Commanding Officer, 7th Armored Division, enters Chartres on August 17, 1944. The M8 armored car carries the markings of the HQ's 26th vehicle. The red plate with the stars of commanding officer is on the right-hand side, above the round plate of the bridge classification.
(National Archives)

Below.
This M20 armored car, entering Montebourg, belongs to the 801st Tank Destroyer Battalion of the First Army. The table on page 45 allows us to see precisely where to find this kind of vehicle within the battalion.
(National Archives)

Below.
An M8 from the 2nd Armored Division, 82nd Cavalry Reconnaissance Squadron, Troop A, enters a German town in early 1945.

Halftrack

Left.
August 21, 1944. Les Hayes, a small hamlet northwest of Tillières-sur-Avres (Eure), where the author resided at the time. Seen here is a halftrack of the 2nd Armored Division, 14th Armored Field Artillery Battalion, C Battery, 1st vehicle.
(J. Bouchery Collection)

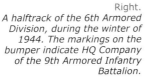

Left.
Normandy, 1944, a wounded German soldier is brought aboard a halftrack, carrying the—partially obliterated by censorship—markings of the 113th Cavalry Reconnaissance Squadron of the First Army.
(National Archives)

Right.
A halftrack of the 6th Armored Division, during the winter of 1944. The markings on the bumper indicate HQ Company of the 9th Armored Infantry Battalion.

Left.
A halftrack of the 756th Tank Battalion of the Seventh Army, near Vesoul, September 1944. This vehicle belongs to Company B's HQ.
(US Army via. C. Routier)

Right.
A local offers a pick-me-up to G.I.s of the 41st Armored Infantry Battalion, 2nd Armored Division. The markings immediately allow us to identify the unit.

Below, left.
12th Armored Division, 112th Armored Engineer Battalion, Rouffach, February 1945. Apart from the indications on the bumper, note the large marking, line and dots, of a light color on the sides of the machine.
(Hackensack U. Library)

Left and above.
A halftrack from an armored unit of the Third Army, during the summer of 1944. Note the placement of the star at the back, the registration and the driving warning for Great Britain.
(National Archives)

Right.
Lorraine, 1944. The wreck of a halftrack from the 25th Cavalry Reconnaissance Squadron, 4th Armored Division, Troop D's 38th vehicle.

M5 Light Tank

The markings on this light tank, photographed during Operation Cobra are visible at the back of the hull: 3rd Armored Division, 33rd Armored Regiment, Company C's 14th machine. The large tactical markings of the division are painted on the sides but do not adhere exactly to regulations (see also page 124).
(National Archives)

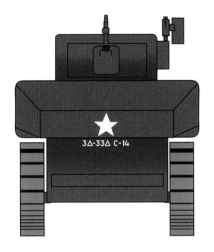

Below.
Light M5A1 tank in Buchet, near Gisors, end of August 1944. The markings are those of the 2nd Armored Division, 66th Armored Regiment, Company A's 7th vehicle.
(US Army via C. Routier)

Another M5 from the 2nd Armored Division in Germany, 1945. This one belongs to the 67th Armored Regiment, Company A's 10th machine.

M4 Medium Tank

Below.
Winter 1944–45 in Belgium. This M32 tank recovery vehicle belongs to 609th Tank Destroyer Battalion's Company C, which was attached to the 10th Armored Division for the duration of the Ardennes campaign. The markings indicate a Third Army unit.
Note the placement of the registration.

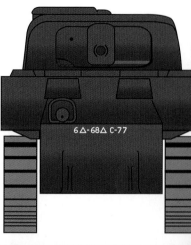

Right.
A Sherman from the 68th Tank Battalion of the 6th Armored Division, Company C's 77th vehicle. Note the large markings on the hull side.

Above.
January 1945 in the Ardennes, an M4 of the 7th Armored Division is being towed by an M26 tractor. The markings at the back of the hull are those of the 31st Tank Battalion, Company B.

Above.
A Sherman from the 14th Armored Division in Germany, 1945. The markings of the 25th Tank Battalion are painted on the barrel. Note the T identifying a tank battalion, rather than the regulation triangle, still present to indicate the division.
(National Archives)

Below.
An M4 tank from the 33rd Armored Regiment, 3rd Armored Division in the Ardennes, late December 1944.

Above.
A Sherman from the 43rd Tank Battalion, 12th Armored Division, armed with a 76mm gun, on a German road with elements of the 63rd Infantry Division.

Below.
A Sherman tankdozer from the 36th Tank Battalion, 8th Armored Division in Germany. As in the case of amphibious tanks (see next page), the markings have been moved to the gun's shield.

M4 Medium Tank

Near Sainte-Mère Église, June 7, 1944. This Duplex Drive (DD) amphibious tank belongs to the 70th Tank Battalion, First Army, assigned to the 4th Infantry Division, who landed the previous day on Utah Beach. Due to the floating device, the unit markings have been moved to the gun shield.

Left.
In Normandy, this Sherman from the 743rd Tank Battalion is the 7th vehicle of the HQ Company. The unit markings are placed on the hood which allowed exhaust fumes to escape in shallow water. This unit was part of the First Army, and accompanied the 29th Infantry Division during the landings.

Below.
Early 1945. On this Sherman from the 735th Tank Battalion, the space on the front being used for a jack and track extensions, and the unit markings have been painted by hand in front of the driver's spot. At that time, the battalion was supporting the 26th Infantry Division, also of the XX Corps.

M8 Howitzer Motor Carriage

Normandy 1944. Seen here is a self-propelled 75mm M8 from the 33rd Armored Regiment, 3rd Armored Division, 16th vehicle of the Reconnaissance Battalion (R-16).

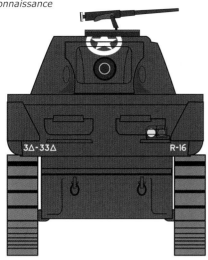

M7 Howitzer Motor Carriage

Right.
England 1944. These self-propelled 105mm M7s from the 22nd Armored Field Artillery Battalion, 4th Armored Division have just received their unit markings, on the turret supporting the 12.7mm antiaircraft machine guns.
(National Archives via J. Gawne)

Below.
November 1944. A self-propelled M7 is being fitted with new tracks. A unit from the Third Army, the 276th Armored Field Artillery Battalion was supporting the 6th Armored Division at the time. The markings at the rear have been guessed at in the bottom right illustration.
(National Archives via J. Gawne)

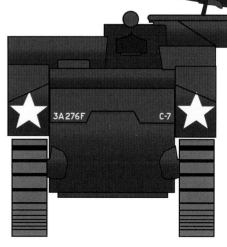

Berlin, 1945. Self-propelled M7s from the 2nd Armored Division fire a volley during a ceremony. At the back of the body can be seen the markings of the 376th Armored Field Artillery Battalion, Battery C.
(National Archives)

M12 Howitzer Motor Carriage

Left.
A 155mm of the 557th Field Artillery Battalion, Third Army, in action during the siege of Brest in August 1944. Note the placement of the stars and the unit markings on the back fenders.
(National Archives via Jon Gawne)

Left.
155mm M12 from the 987th Field Artillery Battalion, First (U.S.) Army, assigned to support the British XXX Corps, early June 1944. The unit markings are at the front, the number 7 being separated from the 98, probably due to a problem fitting the stencil.
(National Archives)

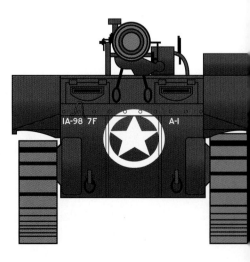

Gun Motor Carriages (Tank Destroyers)

*An M18 Hellcat from the 609th Tank Destroyer Battalion in Germany.
The order of the unit markings is baffling.
The first 9 might refer to Ninth Army, but what about the V?*
(National Archives)

Below, left.
An M10 Gun Motor Carriage in a village in Normandy, June 1944. The markings are those of the 703rd Tank Destroyer Battalion, First Army, which accompanied the 3rd Armored Division in Europe.
(National Archives)

Below, right.
An M18 Hellcat from the 805th Tank Destroyer Battalion, Fifth Army in Italy. The unit markings have been painted by hand on the front of the body. The vehicle number features on the turret.
(National Archives)

AIR FORCES

Right.
A Ninth Air Force airfield in Normandy. The fuel bowser on the 2½-ton truck frame bears the lettering U.S. ARMY AIR FORCES. The markings on the bumper typify aviation markings. The black Ace of Spades identified 9th AF flying units from D-Day onward.

Below.
England, April 1944. This radio-equipped Jeep is from the 391st Bombardment Group, Ninth Air Force. It is painted in a black and yellow checkerboard pattern to accentuate visibility on the runway. Note the light direction indicators at back, to guide heavy bombers into their parking bays.

During World War II, air force units still belonged to the army, made up since reorganization in March 1942 of the Army Ground Forces, Army Service Forces and the Army Air Forces.

The markings of air force vehicles and aircraft were defined by the same AR 850-5 regulations that we have studied in the previous chapters.

Here are some examples of these markings, as well as the peculiarities of the Ninth Air Force, that was charged with supporting ground troops and which also deployed service units, personnel, and vehicles to France in June 1944.

Note: On the bumpers of the air forces' vehicles, the first star was part of the unit markings and identified an air force, here the Eighth or the Ninth (see page 82).

Right.
England, June 6, 1944. These P-47 pilots of the Eighth Air Force rejoin their aircraft. The Jeep carries the markings of the 378th Service Squadron, 79th Service Group. The insignia of the 378th is painted on the windshield's frame. The weapons carrier to the right belongs to the 351st Fighter Squadron of the 353rd Fighter Group. Note the indication of antifreeze protection on the top of the grille, illustrated in color in the top right inset.

PRESTONE 44-45

8★353FG ★ 351FS

Below.
At a former German airfield, in France, air force ground crews wait for donuts distributed by the Red Cross. The weapons carrier carries the markings of the 368th Fighter Group from the Ninth Air Force. Note the Ace of Spades on the bumper, also visible on the tanker on the previous page. The inset uses the example of the 396th Fighter Squadron, one of the three squadrons of the group.

TACTICAL MARKINGS OF THE NINTH AIR FORCE, 1944

Air Force Units	Signals Units	Ordnance Units	Medical Units	Engineer Units	Quartermaster Units	Chemical Units

Before the departure for France, instructions stipulated that the unit markings of the two first groups should be erased and replaced with an Ace of Spades (see left for color coding). The photograph below shows that these instructions were not always followed as the 9 and the star on the bumper are still there with the 368th Fighter Group marking.

♠ 9 ★368FG   396FS-3

Eighth Air Force
1192nd Military Police Company

A IXEC 834E ★ HB 27

Above.
A Diamond T972 dumper truck, from the 834th Aviation Engineer Battalion clearing rubble in the German town of Furth, in 1945. The markings on the bumper start with the Aviation Engineer insignia (inset above), followed by the markings of the IX Engineer Command of the Ninth Air Force, then those of the unit.

Below, left.
Several months earlier, a 2½-ton truck from the same battalion, takes part in an exercise.

Below, right.
Seen here in May 1943, at Bassingbourn airfield in England, is a radio Jeep from the 323rd Bombardment Squadron, 91st Bombardment Group, Eighth Air Force. The gantry assists with B-17 steering during taxiing.

9 ★ 834E ★ ★ B51

8 ★ -91BG -323 -16

At a British base, mechanics from the 830th Aviation Engineers of the Ninth Air Force receive instruction on waterproofing vehicles before the D-Day landings.

Right.
August 17, 1944 in Provence, this is a 2½-ton truck from the 927th Signal Battalion, XII Tactical Air Command of the Twelfth Air Force. Being a signal unit, the color of the orange bands on the bumper is only guessed at.
(National Archives)

Below.
Italy, fall 1944, a 4,000-gallon F1 fuel-servicing bowser is hitched to an Autocar tractor that shows the markings of the 350th Fighter Group of the Twelfth Air Force.
(National Archives)

TACTICAL MARKINGS
Typical of Certain Divisions

43200

A halftrack from the Antitank Platoon of the 2nd Battalion's HQ and HQ Company, 18th Infantry, 1st Division, on a Normandy beach. The circular insignia on the bumper allows us to identify the sub-unit.

According to regulations, the commanding officers of divisions, brigades, and combat teams, were authorized to define their own vehicle markings.

Tactical markings in certain units fulfilled the same function as those described previously, with two exceptions:

- They were reserved for tactical units
- They had to be indecipherable to enemy intelligence, whilst being immediately recognizable by the concerned units' personnel.

These markings took the shape of simple colored stripes and/or geometric shapes, without attracting the attention of the occasional observer. Tactical markings could also include

Previous page, top.
Vehicles from the 1st
Infantry Division's HQ
Company, on board a
landing craft in Normandy.
The unit markings have not
been removed on the white
bumpers. The black star is
the tactical insignia of the
HQ and HQ Company. This
mark, typical of the division
is explained on page 122.
On the right is painted the
unit serial number 43200
and the corresponding
colored stripes. The star
on the hood is painted on
a vesicant-detection yellow
background.

Right.
A GMC reversing into an LST
on its way to Normandy.
The tactical insignia painted
on the star on the door is
unidentified. Perhaps the
Maintenance Ordnance
Company?

other relevant information (for example a common initial for a small unit).

Like the standard markings, they were made with pigments soluble in petrol and their placement was determined by the unit's commanding officer and could be erased if required.

Below, left.
A halftrack from the 16th Infantry Regiment, 1st Infantry Division enters Mons. The circular insignia on the left of the bumper is that of the regiment.

Below, right.
A halftrack of the 16th Infantry Regiment, 1st Infantry Division in Germany. The circular insignia on the body and the 57mm gun indicate that this machine belongs to the Antitank Company.

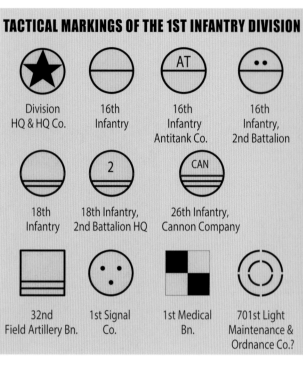

TACTICAL MARKINGS OF THE 1ST INFANTRY DIVISION

Division HQ & HQ Co.	16th Infantry	16th Infantry Antitank Co.	16th Infantry, 2nd Battalion
18th Infantry	18th Infantry, 2nd Battalion HQ	26th Infantry, Cannon Company	
32nd Field Artillery Bn.	1st Signal Co.	1st Medical Bn.	701st Light Maintenance & Ordnance Co.?

Above.
June 1944, England. The yellow and black geometrical marking of the 1st Medical Battalion is visible on the doors and the bumper of this ambulance. Like numerous vehicles of the "Big Red One," the bumper is white and the standard tactical markings are black. A large patch of vesicant-detection paint can be seen on the hood.

Below.
The 32nd Field Artillery Battalion of the 1st Infantry Division also prepares for France. The truck in the background is Battery B's 5th vehicle. The yellow and black tactical sign is reproduced at the center of the white star painted on the tailgate.

Above.
Summary of the geometrical markings of the 1st Infantry Division, used since North Africa and confirmed by the standard markings on the bumpers, preserved despite the instructions given for the D-Day landings. These markings were suppressed by a circular from the division's HQ, dated February 27, 1945.

Presented here is a summary of the markings employed by the 1st Infantry Division since North Africa and by the 29th Infantry Division in Normandy. Other units employed similar markings, but their key is as yet undeciphered.

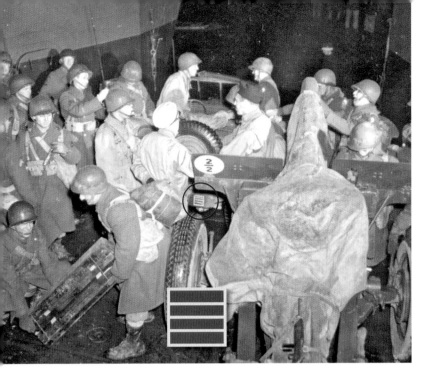

Above.
January 1944 in the south of England, a landing exercise for the 224th Field Artillery Battalion. Note in the middle of the photograph, on one of the Jeep's bumpers, the square tactical marking of this unit from the 29th Infantry Division.
(National Archives)

Above, right.
This M26 Weasel from the 29th Infantry Division is missing its regulation markings, bar the C of the company. The geometric insignia at the front however, lets us identify the 121st Engineer Combat Battalion, as well as the Latin motto of the unit, and the one in French "Essayons" (Let's try) from the U.S. Army Engineers. "Let's go" was the divisional slogan.
(National Archives)

Below.
The Jeep of General Gerhardt, Commanding Officer of the 29th Division, was christened Vixen Tor (on the windshield). On the bumper, other than the red plate with two stars, can be seen the yellow tactical marking that identifies the division's HQ. This vehicle is now kept at the Maryland Museum of Military History.

TACTICAL MARKINGS OF THE 29TH INFANTRY DIVISION

Div. HQ & HQ Co.	104th Med. Battalion	121st Eng. Battalion	Heavy Tank Battalion[1]	29th Recon. Troop
729th Ordnance Co.	29th Signal Co.	29th QM. Co.	129th AAA Bn[2]	
115th Infantry	116th Infantry	175th Infantry		
29th Div. Artillery	110th FA Battalion	111th FA Battalion	224th FA Battalion	227th FA Battalion

Tactical markings defined by the division's HQ before Normandy. 10cm squares, 6mm yellow lines.

[1] This must be a theoretical marking, perhaps for the non-divisional tank battalion, attached to the division for the landings.
[2] Ditto. There was no 129th Antiaircraft Battalion. The division did not have an organic AAA battalion, the one allocated to it being the 459th AAA Automatic Weapons Battalion.

Right.
England, 1944. The marking placement in armored units was non-systematic, with large letters or numbers painted white or yellow on the sides. On this White M3A1 halftrack from the 41st Armored Infantry Regiment, 2nd Armored Division, the 3 could indicate the 3rd Battalion and the 15 the vehicle individual number

Below.
Late December 1944 in the Ardennes, this halftrack armed with an 81mm mortar, carries on its side the tactical markings of the 1st Battalion, 32nd vehicle.

Below.
Germany. The markings painted on the sides identify the 33rd vehicle of the 3rd Battalion's HQ Company.

An M8 armored car from the 82nd Reconnaissance Squadron, 2nd Armored Division, C Troop, 30th. The name of the vehicle that starts with C also indicates C Troop. Colbert is a town in the U.S. state of Georgia.

Lorraine, late December 1944. An M8 captured by the Germans bears the insignia of the 2nd Cavalry Group between the two hatches.

Below.
In the Ardennes, during the winter of 1944/45, G.I.s from the 84th Infantry Division observe Allied bombers. An exception to the rule, and usually forbidden, the division's insignia has been painted in a stylized manner on the left bumper. This Dodge 6x6 is the 10th vehicle of a regimental antitank (AT) company.

Although regulations prohibited insignia that allowed unit identification, infractions were common. The 68th Tank Battalion, amongst others, painted on its tanks an amusing insignia, Toby Tortoise, drawn for them by the Walt Disney Company.

Unit Serial Numbers

Above.
An M7 self-propelled howitzer, from Battery B, 14th Armored Field Artillery Battalion, 2nd Armored Division, June 1944. Its unit serial number is 45570, painted at the front of the body with corresponding color stripes.

Below.
The unit corresponding to no. 51032 is unknown; however, the red Ace of Spades, the triangular insignia on the left bumper and the insignia on the men's shoulders, indicate an engineers battalion from the Ninth Air Force.

This chapter has only been made possible thanks to the patient research conducted in the United States by two enthusiasts: Ben C. Major and Lois S. Montbertrand, whose book is mentioned in the bibliography.

The basic key that led to this important discovery (of unit serial numbers) resided in the Build-up priority tables: numbered lists of the formations and units selected to participate in the D-Day landings and later in the liberation of France. Classified by order of arrival on the continent, these units received a unit serial number.

To ensure the loading of units in the convened order on the tactical transports to France, a five-digit number[1] was allocated to each formation, including basic sub unit level: company, platoon, battery, etc. This number had to be easily visible on all vehicles, artillery pieces, trailers, but also on all unit baggage (packs, footlockers, canteens, various crates).

More than 8,000 numbers were allocated not only to the units involved in D-Day, but also to those which would intervene at a later date in the campaign: thus, list A classified those units which would engage from D-Day to D+14, and list B for those committed from D+15 to D+90.

This code was to ensure utmost secrecy in the troop dispositions during and after the landings.

[1] *This codification already existed with the British B.E.F. of 1939—40 and was used by the U.S. Army after the landings in Sicily.*

[2] *Photographic documents of the time prove that these instructions went unheeded in the most part.*

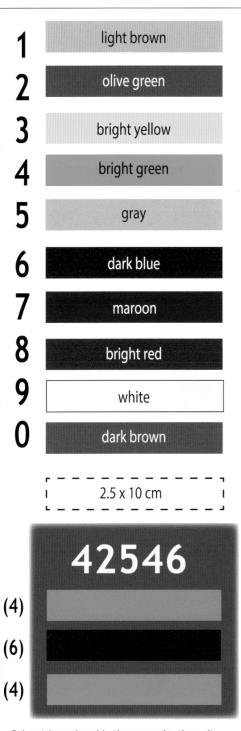

1	light brown
2	olive green
3	bright yellow
4	bright green
5	gray
6	dark blue
7	maroon
8	bright red
9	white
0	dark brown

2.5 x 10 cm

42546

(4)

(6)

(4)

Color stripes placed in threes, under the unit serial number. The top and bottom stripes are of the color of the penultimate digit of the unit number, while the middle stripe is of the color of the last digit.

Above.
An example for the vehicles and baggage of the HQ Company of the 29th Infantry Division, whose number was 42546.

42143

Above.
The unit serial number 42143 and corresponding stripes are visible on the hood of the Jeep on the right, and the duffle bag tied to the fender. These identify a car from the Headquarters & Service Troop, 102nd Cavalry Reconnaissance Squadron.

Below.
A GMC of the 360th Aviation Engineer Battalion in England, 1944. The color stripes are painted on a white background on the left of the bumper, followed by a barely legible serial number on the right of the battalion's emblem. The Lister bag also carries the number and stripes.

Note for the Preparation for Overseas Movement[2] issued to logistics personnel, summed up the rules that had to be applied before the landings:

- Personnel in the units concerned must remove or erase any divisional insignia on all equipment and uniforms.
- Concerning the vehicles, only the following markings should be kept: registration number, national insignia (stars), tonnage and size markings (see page 68), tactical markings of the 3rd and 4th groups (letters designating the company, battery, etc.) and numbers indicating the vehicle's position in the order of march (see chapter 5).

Right.
Normandy, June 1944. This Jeep carries the number 43319 on its back bumper, which identifies the HQ & HQ Battery of the 7th Field Artillery Battalion, 1st Infantry Division. The white bumpers are also a clue to the division's identity.

Stripe Codes

In order to facilitate the identification of vehicles, luggage, and impedimenta during loading and unloading operations, before and after the Channel crossing, a code system with colored stripes was implemented to complete the unit serial number. This code was made up of three horizontal stripes.

To keep the number of colors to a minimum and ease the identification process:

- The color representing the last digit of the unit serial number was used on the middle stripe.
- The color representing the penultimate digit was used for the top and bottom stripes.

The unit serial number was placed above or on the side of these colored stripes, depending on the space available, in principle in black paint, but to make them more legible, these markings could be painted on a 5- x 5-inch white square.

Right.
This Sherman Rhino bears the color stripes corresponding to unit serial number 44106, from the 503rd Ordnance Heavy Maintenance Company. This unit is said to have been the originator of the hedge-cutting Rhino device, that allowed tanks to penetrate the thick Norman hedgerows. The markings above the color stripes are those of the 747th Tank Battalion, First Army, which received the machine in Normandy.

Below.
England, early June 1944. These M4 tractors carry on the front left the code 43933, which designates the 955th Field Artillery Battalion, armed with 155mm howitzers. This First Army unit was attached in support of the 29th Infantry Division.

Below.
Despite the efforts of the censor, the usual unit markings are still legible on the fenders.

45134

46617

Above.
In this photograph taken before loading in June 1944, we can read on the jeep bumperette the number 45134, which was a little-known unit, the 293rd Joint Assault Signal Company (Jasco).

Above, right.
Number 46617, painted at the back of this 1-ton water tank, is that of the 45th Field Hospital.

Below.
Number 51198, painted on the left side of this truck's tailgate, is that of the 834th Aviation Engineer Battalion, Company C.

43150

51198

Above.
This M29 is the 27th vehicle of the HQ Company, 146th Engineer Combat Battalion in June 1944. The code 43150, barely legible on the left of the photograph, is confirmed by the usual unit markings.

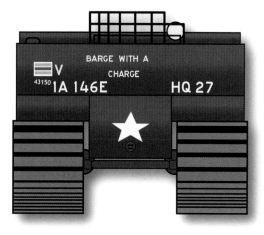

Above.
An M8 armored car from the 4th Cavalry Reconnaissance Squadron's Troop B, 4th Cavalry Group, identified by the unit markings at the front, confirmed by the number 44883. The corresponding color stripes are painted on the opposite side.

Right.
Bataan was an M36 from the 603rd Tank Destroyer Battalion (SP), Company B, in Brittany during the summer of 1944. The unit number—probably 47997—and the color stripes are painted at the side front.
(National Archives via J. Gawne)

Right.
General Patton's M20 armored car bears the flag of his rank and unit serial number 48623. Although the key to the serial numbers of units that arrived after D+14—amongst whom was the Third Army—is unknown, we can surmise that 48623 corresponds to the HQ & HQ Company of Patton's Third Army. The color for the 2 is identical to the green of the vehicle, so these two stripes are outlined in white.

48623

Below.
Cannoneer was a Sherman from the 743rd Tank Battalion's Company C in Normandy, in early June 1944. The unit serial number, 43987 is painted on the front plate, above the corresponding maroon/red stripes, and next to the usual unit markings (see illustration on page 135). The battalion was a First Army unit. The flag label that attests to the waterproofing of the tank (see page 71) has been stuck in front of the driver's hatch.
(National Archives)

43987

SELECTION OF UNIT SERIAL NUMBERS FOR THE UNITS THAT LANDED BETWEEN

NON-DIVISIONAL UNITS

 31890
1st Engineer Special Brigade, 577th Quartermaster Battalion, Headquarters Company

 46074
635th Tank Destroyer Battalion, A Company (attached to the 1st Infantry Division)

 43559
741st Tank Battalion, Independent (Duplex Drive), A Company (attached to the 1st Infantry Division)

 42356
803rd Tank Destroyer Battalion, C Company (attached to the 3rd Armored Division)

 44034
70th Tank Battalion Headquarters & Headquarters Company (attached to the 4th Infantry Division)

 44345
457th Antiaircraft Artillery Battalion, A Battery (attached to the 29th Infantry Division)

 44042
743rd Tank Battalion, D Company (attached to the 29th Infantry Division)

45696
746th Tank Battalion, Headquarters & Headquarters Company (attached to the 90th Infantry Division)

1st INFANTRY DIVISION

 43370
1st Infantry Division, 16th Infantry Regiment, 1st Battalion, Headquarters & Headquarters Company

 43362
1st Infantry Division, 16th Infantry Regiment, C Company

 43372
1st Infantry Division, 16th Infantry Regiment, 3rd Battalion, Headquarters & Headquarters Company

 43357
1st Infantry Division, 16th Infantry Regiment, Antitank Company

 43392
1st Infantry Division, 18th Infantry Regiment, 1st Battalion, Headquarters & Headquarters Company

 43394
1st Infantry Division, 18th Infantry Regiment, 3rd Battalion, Headquarters & Headquarters Company

 43397
1st Infantry Division, 18th Infantry Regiment, I Company

43377
1st Infantry Division, 18th Infantry Regiment, Antitank Company

1st INFANTRY DIVISION

 43503
1st Infantry Division, 26th Infantry Regiment, 1st Battalion, Headquarters & Headquarters Company

 43494
1st Infantry Division, 26th Infantry Regiment, L Company

 43505
1st Infantry Division, 26th Infantry Regiment, 3rd Battalion, Headquarters & Headquarters Company

43468
1st Infantry Division, 26th Infantry Regiment, Medical Detachment

4th INFANTRY DIVISION

 45844
4th Infantry Division, 8th Infantry Regiment, 1st Battalion, Headquarters & Headquarters Company

 45834
4th Infantry Division, 8th Infantry Regiment, 1st Battalion, Headquarters & Headquarters Company

 45824
4th Infantry Division, 8th Infantry Regiment, 3rd Battalion, Headquarters & Headquarters Company

 45793
4th Infantry Division, 8th Infantry Regiment, A Company

Based on Major & Montbertrand, First Army Build-Up (priority tables, list A, D+1 through D+14), *WW2 US Medical Research Center 2011*

JUNE 6 AND 20, 1944
4th INFANTRY DIVISION

45827 — 4th Infantry Division, 12th Infantry Regiment, Headquarters & Headquarters Company

45820 — 4th Infantry Division, 12th Infantry Regiment, 1st Battalion, Headquarters & Headquarters Company

45810 — 4th Infantry Division, 12th Infantry Regiment, 2nd Battalion, Headquarters & Headquarters Company

45853 — 4th Infantry Division, 12th Infantry Regiment, 2nd Battalion, Headquarters & Headquarters Company

45823 — 4th Infantry Division, 12th Infantry Regiment, K Company

45594 — 4th Infantry Division, 22nd Infantry Regiment, 1st Battalion, Headquarters & Headquarters Company

45609 — 4th Infantry Division, 22nd Infantry Regiment, Antitank Company

45610 — 4th Infantry Division, 22nd Infantry Regiment, Cannon Company

EXAMPLES OF UNIT SERIAL NUMBER PLACEMENT

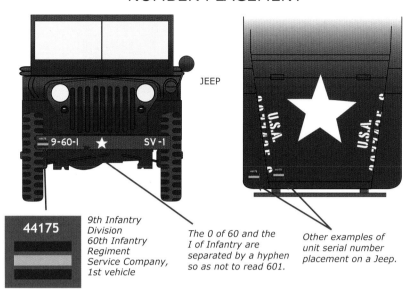

JEEP

9-60-I   ★   SV-1

44175 — 9th Infantry Division 60th Infantry Regiment Service Company, 1st vehicle

The 0 of 60 and the I of Infantry are separated by a hyphen so as not to read 601.

Other examples of unit serial number placement on a Jeep.

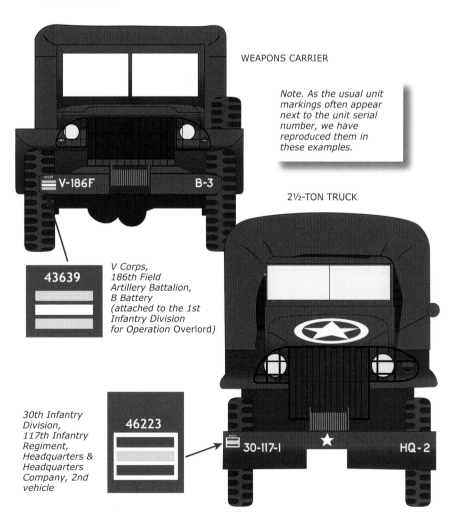

WEAPONS CARRIER

Note. As the usual unit markings often appear next to the unit serial number, we have reproduced them in these examples.

V-186F   B-3

43639 — V Corps, 186th Field Artillery Battalion, B Battery (attached to the 1st Infantry Division for Operation Overlord)

2½-TON TRUCK

30-117-I   ★   HQ-2

46223 — 30th Infantry Division, 117th Infantry Regiment, Headquarters & Headquarters Company, 2nd vehicle

SELECTION OF UNIT SERIAL NUMBERS FOR THE UNITS THAT LANDED BETWEEN

29th INFANTRY DIVISION

 42587 — 29th Infantry Division, 115th Infantry Regiment, Headquarters & Headquarters Company

 42904 — 29th Infantry Division, 115th Infantry Regiment, Antitank Company

 42376 — 29th Infantry Division, 116th Infantry Infantry, Medical Detachment

 42458 — 29th Infantry Division, 175th Infantry Regiment, K Company

 42705 — 29th Infantry Division, 104th Medical Battalion, C Company

 42638 — 29th Infantry Division, 224th Field Artillery Battalion, Service Battery

 42348 — 29th Infantry Division, 234th Engineer Combat Battalion, A Company (attached for June 6)

 43016 — 29th Infantry Division, Military Intelligence Detachment, Counter-Intelligence Corps

90th INFANTRY DIVISION

 46804 — 90th Infantry Division, Divisional Artillery, Headquarters & Headquarters Battery

 46699 — 90th Infantry Division, 357th Infantry Regiment, C Company

 46718 — 90th Infantry Division, 357th Infantry Regiment, Service Company

 46742 — 90th Infantry Division, 358th Infantry Regiment, M Company

 46810 — 90th Infantry Division, 315th Engineer Combat Battalion, B Company

 46788 — 90th Infantry Division, 344th Field Artillery Battalion, C Battery

 46690 — 90th Infantry Division, Military Police Platoon

47337 — 90th Infantry Division, Band

2nd ARMORED DIVISION

 44486 — 2nd Armored Division, 41st Armored Infantry Regiment, B Company

44508 — 2nd Armored Division, 66th Armored Regiment, 3rd Battalion, Headquarters & Headquarters Company

44510 — 2nd Armored Division, 67th Armored Regiment, Maintenance Company

44470 — 2nd Armored Division, Division trains, Maintenance Battalion, C Company

3rd ARMORED DIVISION

42870 — 3rd Armored Division, 32nd Armored Regiment, C Company

 42766 — 3rd Armored Division, 36th Armored Infantry Regiment, B Company

 42954 — 3rd Armored Division, 23rd Armored Engineer Battalion, A Company

42832 — 3rd Armored Division, 67th Armored Field Artillery Battalion, A Battery

Based on Major & Montbertrand, First Army Build-Up (priority tables, list A, D+1 through D+14), *WW2 US Medical Research Center 2011*

82nd AIRBORNE DIVISION

 44636 — 82nd Airborne Division, Headquarters & Headquarters Company

 44652 — 82nd Airborne Division, 505th Parachute Infantry Regiment

 44443 — 82nd Airborne Division, 507th Parachute Infantry Regiment

 44868 — 82nd Airborne Division, 508th Parachute Infantry Regiment

 44614 — 82nd Airborne Division, 325th Glider Infantry Regiment, Service Company

 44630 — 82nd Airborne Division, Divisional Artillery Headquarters

 44612 — 82nd Airborne Division, 319th Glider Field Artillery Battalion, Headquarters & Service Battery

 44633 — 82nd Airborne Division, 80th Airborne Anti Aircraft Artillery Battalion, E Battery

101st AIRBORNE DIVISION

 42289 — 101st Airborne Division, Headquarters & Headquarters Company

 45641 — 101st Airborne Division, 501st Parachute Infantry Regiment, Headquarters Company

 43040 — 101st Airborne Division, 502nd Parachute Infantry Regiment, H Company

 42353 — 101st Airborne Division, 506th Parachute Infantry Regiment, C Company

 42151 — 101st Airborne Division, 506th Parachute Infantry Regiment, D Company

 42094 — 101st Airborne Division, 327th Glider Infantry Regiment

 43102 — 101st Airborne Division, 326th Airborne Engineer Battalion, B Company

 42165 — 101st Airborne Division, 321st Glider Field Artillery Battalion

EXAMPLES OF UNIT SERIAL NUMBER PLACEMENT

M20 ARMORED UTILITY CAR

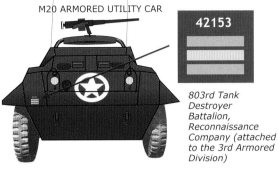

42153 — 803rd Tank Destroyer Battalion, Reconnaissance Company (attached to the 3rd Armored Division)

M5 LIGHT TANK

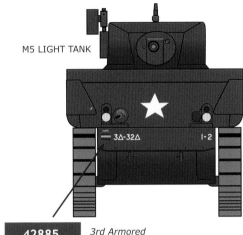

 42885 — 3rd Armored Division. 32nd Armored Regiment I Company

743rd Tank Battalion, separate, C Company, see page 123

43987

M4 MEDIUM TANK

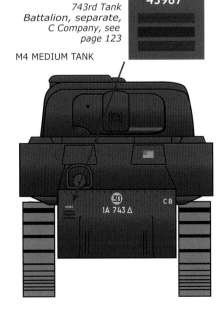

6 CAMOUFLAGE

An M15 halftrack from the 441st AAA (AW) Battalion on Camel Red Beach, during the landings in Provence. The camouflage is made up of black patches on a green background, as per model F on the next page.

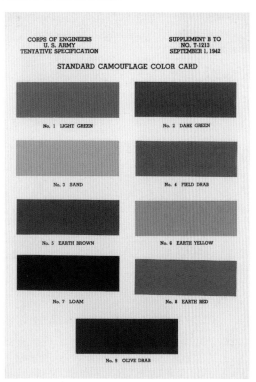

CORPS OF ENGINEERS U. S. ARMY TENTATIVE SPECIFICATION	SUPPLEMENT B TO NO. T-1213 SEPTEMBER 1, 1942

STANDARD CAMOUFLAGE COLOR CARD

No. 1 LIGHT GREEN	No. 2 DARK GREEN
No. 3 SAND	No. 4 FIELD DRAB
No. 5 EARTH BROWN	No. 6 EARTH YELLOW
No. 7 LOAM	No. 8 EARTH RED
No. 9 OLIVE DRAB	

This chapter is adapted from a study by the Corps of Engineers in 1942, preparatory to overseas operations. In 1944, Olive Drab, color No. 9 on the card at left, was the standard color for all equipment.

The camouflage of the vehicles in the field with the help of mud, or with grease mixed with sand, is of the highest importance in combat, where the success of the mission can depend on discretion, and where one must be able to find, locally, a quickly prepared and easily applied medium.

The mud is obtained by mixing soil with water in a pail; it is then smeared on the vehicle or even poured onto it. The soil must be of the characteristic color of the area where the vehicle is operating, and the mud, once dry, must have the same qualities. The camouflage colors can be changed to

Opposite page.

CAMOUFLAGE PATTERNS

A. Model suggested for warm zones and the jungle. Overall and detailed views of a medium tank painted in three colors. Two or three colors are enough to realize a standard camouflage in these regions.

B. The patches must be in proportion and adapted to the shape of the vehicle. The patches in figure A aim to prevent the distinction of shapes, whilst the camouflage in figure B has the opposite effect.

C. Using strong colors and avoiding neat lines, the color patches hide the shapes better if they envelop the angles, or avoid making vulnerable points visible.

D. Three colors have been used on this Olive Drab halftrack: dark brown and black on the hood, white on the wheels and tracks. When this vehicle is in the open, this kind of camouflage blends with the terrain.

E. The most efficient method is to use strong contrasts, but the placement of the contours and vulnerable points becomes harder to get right.

F. As a rule of thumb, use black in moderation, as earth is rarely black or even dark, apart from occasional rocky ground.

G. Contrast of three colors used on a self-propelled M7. The black is used to simulate shadows, with white on the tracks, whilst the rest is painted in the terrain's dominant color.

WRONG

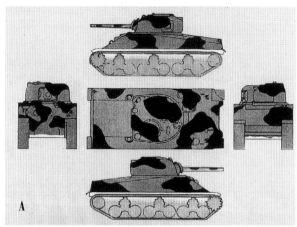

A

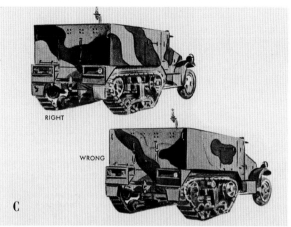

RIGHT

WRONG

C

RIGHT

WRONG

E

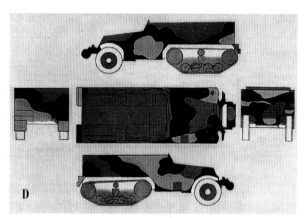

D

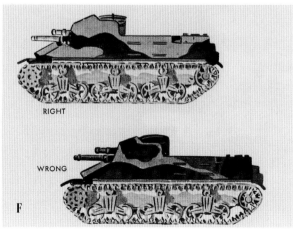

RIGHT

WRONG

F

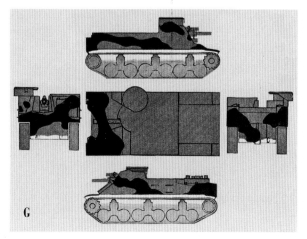

G

H. Patterns suggested for a desert terrain. Camouflage with large patches in two colors used on an M10, operating on ground with strong undulations.

I. On a dominantly red desert terrain, the 75mm M3 tank destroyer would appear very indistinct thanks to its two color patches.

J. Suggested pattern for snowy terrain, which allows a truck to blend in with a background of snow and trees. Note that the pattern extends to the wheels of the vehicle.

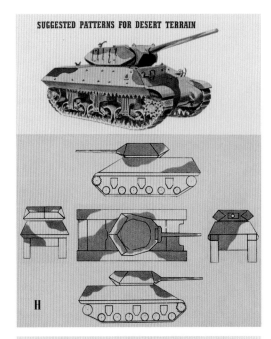

SUGGESTED PATTERNS FOR DESERT TERRAIN

H

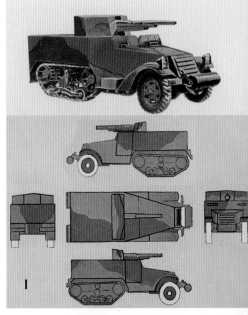

I

In the ETO, vehicles and equipment were actually camouflaged only during the winter of 1944.

Right.
A Jeep camouflaged in white; the unit marking on the bumper has been erased.

Below.
February 1945, on the plains around Colmar, Shermans advance with the 75th Infantry Division. They probably belong to the 5th Armored Division. The whitewash has been applied over the Olive Drab in order to create patches, or wide streaks, like the two M4s on the right of the photograph.
(National Archives)

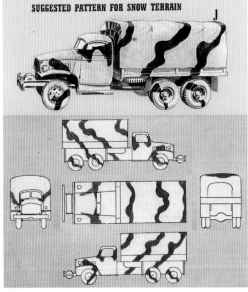

SUGGESTED PATTERN FOR SNOW TERRAIN

J

adapt to the changing landscapes of the operational sector. Camouflaging vehicles on the ground should be part of the units' instructions, but should not be an excuse for poorly maintained equipment when camouflage is not required.

Paint is the most durable way to camouflage vehicles. For better results, oleoresin emulsion paint is recommended, mixing one part of this pigmented paste with one part of water, petrol or white spirit; a ready-to-use oil-based paint is also an option.

In the case of a temporary camouflage, the following products are satisfactory, except in very cold weather, where only the second option is usable:

1. Cold water paint, with a protein-binding agent, obtained by mixing two parts pigment with one part water (or 1.5 kg pigment for 3.8 l water). Some surfaces may require a thicker mixture.

2. Petrol-soluble paint (the one specified for unit markings) with a mix of one part pigment for one part petrol. This product can be removed with a petrol-soaked cloth.

3. Bitumen-emulsion: two parts paste for one part water.

All these products can be applied directly without the use of a primer.

In a snow environment, tarpaulins and soft hoods of the vehicles are covered by brush with water-based white paint (12.5 kg of powder for 2.5 l of water).

Metallic surfaces are covered with either an oleoresin or casein-based paint, also by brush (one and a half part paint for one part petrol).

It takes about six hours to camouflage a 2½-ton truck in white with a brush.

In desert areas, camouflage patterns must extend to the angles and extremities. Their size must also be adapted to the distance at which the vehicle might be spotted. Usually three colors at the most are necessary. A selected combination of the regulatory camouflage colors—earth yellow, earth red, sand, olive drab and black—is enough.

Regulation AR 850-5 section III paragraph 10 stipulates that "when the necessity of camouflage and dissimulation is more important than the identification, the national symbol [the white star] can be erased or covered with a camouflage net, grease, soil or olive drab paint, soluble with petrol."

All these paints are of the type approved by the engineers.

Appendix 1

Material not used by the U.S. Army in 1944–1945

Just as the M201 French Hotchkiss Jeep, even covered in white stars, has no legitimacy in representing the U.S. Army, some restored vehicles have no place at shows or military museums.

This of course does not mean that those vehicles or machines hold no value, but simply that for the most part these were models that, although American-built, were only employed by the British, Soviet or French armies in 1944–45, or else supplied to the French army in the period after the war.

Concerning tanks—and apart from those destroyed in the fighting of 1944–45 and left in situ for commemoration—some AFVs on exhibition in museums, at various monuments or reenactments, were built after the considered period, or have had major modifications, often affecting their physical appearance.

We wish to thank Dr Pierre Clavel, notorious Sherman specialist, who through the Musée des Blindés de Saumur, has brought light on to the transformations made by the French army from 1946 onwards.

Note that the materials donated by the French Army to municipalities or collector groups, often retained their French Army green livery, specified in the notes of May 1959. This color is a lot lighter than the American Olive Drab, which can be observed on the materials delivered from 1950 as part of the military assistance attached to the formation of NATO.

Below.
The White scout car was removed from most organization tables of the U.S. Army in September 1943. Replaced by M8 or M20 armored cars, in 1944–45, it could only display the markings of the British Army, the French Liberation Army (including the 2nd DB—division blindée, or armored division) and the Red Army. The only American units that were allocated this vehicle in Northwest Europe were in theory the Military Police battalions at army level (see page 47).

HALFTRACKS

Halftracks produced by International Harvester, models M5 and M9 are easily recognizable thanks to their flat front fenders, the profile of the doors with an angle cutout near the tracks, and to the rounded angle at the back of the body. Their parts, incompatible with M3 halftracks, were only supplied to Allied nations and therefore they cannot bear U.S. markings of 1944–45.

The M3 White / Autocar / Diamond halftrack has rounded fenders at the front and the back of the body is square. It was exclusively allocated to the U.S. Army.

M5

M3

M5

M3

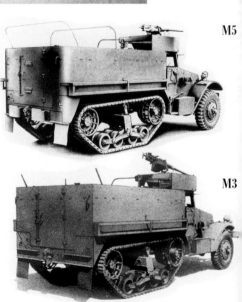

SHERMAN TANKS

1. *Previously displayed as a "flowerpot" in front of the Airborne Museum of Sainte-Mère Église in Normandy, this model saw no combat whatsoever in World War II. It is an M4A1 (76) E8, HVSS suspension, with a cast hull and an aviation radial-type engine, supplied in 1950 to NATO, as part of the U.S. Military Aid Plan. In 2017, it was replaced by an M4A4, which could only display the markings of the British Army or the 1st and 5th French DBs.*

2. *The M4A3 (76) E8, with a welded hull and a Ford V8 engine. It was—along with the 105mm howitzer-armed mid-series M4— the only model equipped with the HVSS undercarriage in the U.S. Army in 1945. It was the star of the movie* Fury. *Note that the 76mm guns were only equipped with a muzzle brake at the end of 1944–early 1945.*

3. *This M4 cannot represent the U.S. Army of 1944. It is an M4A4, driven by a Chrysler A57 multibank engine. This disposition necessitated an extension of the body which entailed spacing out the bogies more than on other models. The M4A4 was not adopted by the U.S. Army due to the difficulty in tuning its engines. Apart from the 2nd DB to which it was not issued, it was widely allocated to the French Liberation Army (1st and 5th DBs) as well as to the British Army. Displayed near Omaha Beach, this M4A4 is in fact a replica built by the French army which has been equipped not only with an episcope cupola, but also with a radial Continental engine, aviation type, meant for M4s and M4A1s. These machines then took the designation M4A4 T.*

4. *and* **5.** *Note the reduced space between the bogies and the wheels on the M4, M4A1, M4A2 and M4A3. The difference with image 3 is obvious.*

Appendix 2: Miscellaneous Markings

The tire pressure (TP) was usually painted white on the dashboard, at the same time as the speed limit (left-hand photograph), but it could sometimes be observed on the body.

In the right-hand image, we can see the camouflage with black patches, but also on the right, one of the two cherry-colored air–ground (AP-50) identification textile panels, which were part of the kit.

Appendix 3: Authorized Abbreviations

AA	Antiaircraft	FA	Field Artillery	P & A	Pioneer & Ammunition
AAA	Antiaircraft Artillery	FAC	Forward Air Controller	Pion	Pioneer
ABN	Airborne	FDC	Fire Direction Center	PIR	Parachute Infantry Regiment
AG	Adjudant General	FO	Forward Observer	Plat	Platoon
AGF	Army Ground Forces	Fwd	Forward	POL	Petroleum, Oil & Lubricants
ALO	Air Liaison Officer			Prcht	Parachute
Amb	Ambulance	G-1 (2,3,4)	General Staff section(s)	Ptbl	Portable
Ammo	Ammunition	GIR	Glider Infantry Regiment		
Amph	Amphibious			QM	Quartermaster
À/car	Armored car	H&S	Headquarters & Service		
Armd	Armored	HH	Headquarters &	Rad	Radio
Arty	Artillery		Headquarters	Rcn	Reconnaissance
AT	Antitank	HHS	HQ, HQ & Service	Recon	Reconnaissance
Autmv	Automotive	How	Howitzer	Rgt	Regiment
AW	Automatic weapons	Hq (HQ)	Headquarters	Rkt	Rocket
		Hvy	Heavy	RO	Reconnaissance Officer
BC	Battery Commander				
BG	Brigadier General	I & R	Intelligence & Reconnaissance	S-1 (2,3,4)	Staff section(s)
Bde	Brigade	Inf	Infantry	Sct	Scout
Bn	Battalion	Intel	Intelligence	Sect	Section
Btry	Battery			Sig.	Signal
		Ldr	Leader	SigC	Signal Corps
C&R	Command & Reconnaissance	Ln O	Liaison Officer	Slt	Searchlight
Cav	Cavalry	Lt	Light	Smbl	Semi-mobile
CC	Combat command	LZ	Landing Zone	SP	Self-propelled
Cfr	Chauffeur			Sqd	Squad
CG	Commanding General	MAC	Medical Administrative Corps	Sqdn	Squadron
Ch	Chief	Maint	Maintenance	Sur	Surgeon
CM	Counter-mortar				
CO	Commanding Officer	Med	Medical	TCG	Troop Carrier Group
Co	Company	Met	Meteorological	TCS	Troop Carrier Squadron
CofS	Chief of Staff	MG	Major General	TCW	Troop Carrier Wing
COL	Colonel	MO	Medical Officer	Tg	Telegraph
COE	Cab over engine	Mort	Mortar	Tk	Tank
Com	Communication	Mot	Motor	Tlr	Trailer
Cmd	Command	MP	Military Police	Topo	Topography, Topographic
Cmdr	Commander	Msg Ctr	Message Center	Tp	Telephone
CP	Command Post	Msgr	Messenger	Trac	Tractor
		Mtcl	Motorcycle	Trk	Truck
DC	Dental Corps	Mtd	Mounted	Trp	Troop
Demo	Demolitions	Mtr	Motor	TT	Teletype
Det	Detachment	Mun	Munitions		
Div	Division			Veh	Vehicle
DS	Direct Support	O	Observer		
DZ	Drop Zone	Obsv	Observation	Wkr	Wrecker
		OP	Observation Post	Wpn	Weapon
Engr	Engineer	Ops	Operations		
Equip	Equipment	Ord	Ordnance	XO	Executive Officer

Sources & Bibliography

OFFICIAL SOURCES

AR 850-5 (Army Regulations) August 5, 1942, US Military Equipment Markings.
Technical Manual TM 9-2800 Standard Military Motor Vehicles, September 1, 1943, pdf Google books
TM 9-2800. Ministère de la guerre. Véhicules automobiles militaires. September 25, 1943
AR 850-10 change 1, Registration of Motor Vehicles, November 5, 1942
AR-850-150 Authorized Abbreviations and symbols, September 1944 & January 1945
Unit Citation and Campaign Participation Credit Register, DA Pamphlet 672-2, HQ DA July 1961
Dictionary of US Army Terms, SR 320-1-5, DA November 1953
AR 260-10 Flags, colors, standards and guidons

OTHER SOURCES

Books in French

US Army 1944–1945. Marquages et organisation. Emile Becker & Jean Milmeister. Luxembourg 1988
Les roues de la Liberté, Nicolas Aubin, Histoire & Collections, 2014
Les paras américains du D-Day. C. Deschodt & L. Rouger. Histoire & Collections, 2004
Militaria magazine. Histoire et Collections: suite d'articles rédigés par Jean-Michel Boniface
Jour J à l'aube. Jonathan Gawne. Histoire et Collections, 1998
U.S Army Photo Album, Jonathan Gawne. Histoire et Collections, 1996
Allied Liberation Vehicles. François Bertin. Editions Ouest-France, 2004
L'Armored Car Ford M8-M20. Patrick Sarrazin. Ps Editions, 2013
GI-Government issue. Guide du collectionneur. HP Enjames. Histoire et Collections, 2003
Guide Militaria n° 6, Les insignes tissu de l'armée américaine, par Pierre Besnard, Histoire et Collections, 2006
Ça sentait bon la liberté et l'espérance, histoire de la libération de Digne, 14–20 août 1944, par Guy S. Reymond, éd. Les petites affiches, Digne les bains, 1993
Les Halftracks US, du M2 au M9, Didier Andres, Regiarm, 2015

Books in English

Finding Your Father's War. Jonathan Gawne. Casemate Publishing, Philadelphia, 2006
Unit Serial Numbers. Ben C. Major & Lois Montbertrand. US Medical Research Centre, 2011
US Tank Destroyers of WW2. Malcolm A. Bellis, 1992
American Enterprise in Europe. Historical section US Army. 1945 (French translation)
US Army Handbook 1939–1945. George Forty, Ian Allan ltd, 1979
Tables of Organization and Equipment WWII (series). J.J. Hays. Printing Services London, 2002
Military Vehicle Markings. Terence Wise, P. Stephens, 1981
American Military Camouflage and Markings 1939–1945. Terence Wise. Almark Publications, 1973
D-Day to Berlin. Camouflage and Markings, USA. British and German Armies. Terence Wise. Arms and Armour Press, 1979
The World War II Soldier's Guide 1943. George Petersen, National Capital Historical Sales
The American Arsenal. Ian V. Hogg. Greenhill Books. London, 1996
US Armor-Cavalry 1917–1967. Duncan Crow. Profile Publications Ltd, 1973
Red Ball Express. Pat Ware. Ian Allan Publishing, 2008, Vols I & II. Collection Tankograd. Michael Franz, Verlag Jochen Vollert
ETO Logistical Support of the Armies, Vol. II, Roland G. Ruppenthal, Office of the Chief of Military History, Washington DC, 1959
Order of Battle World War Two US Army, Shelby Stanton, Presidio Press 1984
WW2 Data Book, John Ellis, Aurum Press, 1993
The Big Macks, a visual history of the Mack wheeled prime movers in Army service 1940–1958, David Doyle, Ampersand group, 2014
The Army Air Forces in WW2, Vol. III, Europe:Argument to VE-Day, W.F. Craven & J.L. Cate

WEBSITES

WW2 radio Facebook page
www.theliberator.be

Published in the United States of America and Great Britain in 2019 by
CASEMATE PUBLISHERS
1950 Lawrence Road, Havertown, PA 19083, USA
and
The Old Music Hall, 106–108 Cowley Road, Oxford OX4 1JE, UK

This book is published in cooperation with and under license from Sophia His-
toire & Collections. Originally published in French as
U.S. Army 1944 Les marquages des vehicules © Histoire & Collections 2018
Typeset and design © Casemate Publishers 2019
Translation by Myriam Bell
Edited by Chris Cocks
Design by Myriam Bell Design
Original graphics and design by Philippe Charbonnier and Michael Klein

Hardcover Edition: ISBN 978-1-61200-7373
Digital Edition: ISBN 978-1-61200-7380

A CIP record for this book is available from the British Library

Printed and bound in the Czech Republic by FINIDR, s.r.o.

For a complete list of Casemate titles, please contact:

CASEMATE PUBLISHERS (US)
Telephone (610) 853-9131
Fax (610) 853-9146
Email: casemate@casematepublishers.com
www.casematepublishers.com

CASEMATE PUBLISHERS (UK)
Telephone (01865) 241249
Email: casemate-uk@casematepublishers.co.uk
www.casematepublishers.co.uk